PHPEXPRESS

Fast-Track Your Mastery

of

DYNAMIC

WEB

DEVELOPMENT

Daniel D

Contents

Chapter 1: Introduction to PHP and Setting up a Development Environment

I am thrilled that you have chosen this book to enhance your PHP skills and embark on a journey of dynamic web programming.

In this book, I have curated a comprehensive collection of topics that will give you a thorough understanding of PHP, without overwhelming you with unnecessary details. By the end of this book, not only will you have a solid grasp of the language, but you will also have the opportunity to put your knowledge to the test by building a dynamic website together.

As you begin this journey, it's important to note that a basic understanding of HTML and MySQL is required to fully grasp the concepts presented in this book.

Are you ready to dive into the world of PHP and start creating dynamic web applications? Let's get started!

1.1 Overview of PHP

PHP is a popular server-side scripting language used to build dynamic web applications. It stands for Hypertext Preprocessor and it is an open-source programming language, which means it is free to use and modify.

PHP was created in 1995 by Rasmus Lerdorf and it has evolved over the years to become one of the most widely-used programming languages for web development. PHP is particularly well-suited for building dynamic, database-driven websites. It can be used to create a wide variety of web applications, from simple contact forms to complex content management systems and e-commerce platforms.

1.2 Setting up a Local Development Environment

To start developing PHP applications, you will need a web server and a PHP engine installed on your computer. There are several options available to set up a local development environment for PHP.

The most popular options are:

• XAMPP: is a free and open-source package that includes the Apache web server, PHP, and a database management system (MySQL)

• WAMP: is similar to XAMPP and it also includes Apache, PHP, and MySQL

• LAMP: is another popular option, which includes Linux, Apache, PHP, and MySQL

• MAMP: is the MacOS version of the LAMP stack

Each of these packages includes everything you need to run PHP scripts on your local machine. Once you have installed the package of your choice, you can start writing PHP scripts and test them on your local machine.

1.3 Understanding the Role of a Web Server and PHP Engine

When it comes to creating dynamic web applications, one of the key components is the web server. A web server is a software that receives requests from clients (such as a web browser) and sends back the appropriate responses. The most popular web servers are Apache and NGINX.

In addition to the web server, PHP also plays a crucial role in dynamic web development. PHP is a server-side scripting language that is used to create dynamic web pages and applications. When a client sends a request to the web server, the PHP engine interprets the PHP code and generates the appropriate HTML or other output to be sent back to the client.

It's important to note that PHP code is executed on the server, not on the client's device. This means that the client only receives the output of the PHP script, not the actual PHP code. This allows for increased security and flexibility in web development, as sensitive information can be kept on the server and not exposed to the client.

In summary, the web server and PHP engine work together to create dynamic web applications. The web server handles the communication between the client and the server, while the PHP engine processes the PHP code and generates the appropriate output. Together, they make it possible for web developers to create interactive and dynamic websites and applications that can respond to user input and data.

There are other server-side scripting languages such as Python and Ruby, but PHP is particularly well-suited for web development due to its ease of use and wide range of built-in functions and libraries.

In this book, we will be focusing on using PHP as the server-side scripting language to build dynamic web applications. As you progress through the chapters, you will learn how to use PHP to interact with databases, process form data, and create interactive user experiences. With a solid understanding of the role of the web server and PHP engine, you will be well-equipped to start creating dynamic web applications of your own.

1.4 Basic PHP file structure and syntax

A basic PHP file consists of a combination of HTML and PHP code. PHP code is enclosed within special tags `<?php` and `?>`, and can be mixed in with HTML code. For example, the following code would output the text "Hello, world!" within an HTML heading:

```html
<!DOCTYPE html>
<html>
<head>
  <title>My first PHP script</title>
</head>
<body>
  <h1>
    <?php
      echo "Hello, world!";
    ?>
  </h1>
</body>
</html>
```

The above script starts with a standard HTML document, which is then followed by PHP code. The PHP code is enclosed in the tags `<?php` and `?>`, and it will output the text "Hello, world!" when the script is run.

You can write any number of PHP statements within the PHP tags, and the PHP engine will execute them one after the other.

Chapter 2: Basic Syntax, Data Types, and Variables

2.1 Basic Syntax and Structure of a PHP Script

A PHP script is a plain text file that contains a series of PHP commands. The file extension for PHP scripts is typically `.php`, but it can also be `.phtml`, `.php3`, or `.php4`. PHP scripts are executed on the server-side, which means that the client's web browser never sees the raw PHP code; it only receives the output of the script.

2.2 Data Types

PHP supports several data types, including:

• Strings: A sequence of characters enclosed in single or double quotes.

Example: $name = "John";

• Integers: Whole numbers, positive or negative.

Example: $age = 25;

• Floats: Numbers with decimal points.

Example: $price = 3.99;

• Booleans: A data type that can only have two values: true or false.

Example: $isStudent = true;

• Arrays: A collection of values that can be accessed by an index or key.

Example: $colors = array("red", "green", "blue");

• Objects: A special data type

Example:
```
$book = new class {
    public $title;
    public $author;
    public $year;
};
```

In this case, we create an anonymous class and assign its instance to the `$book` variable.

2.3 Constants and Variables

In PHP, constants and variables are two types of storage locations used to hold data. They have some similarities and some differences.

A constant is a value that cannot be changed once it has been defined. Constants are defined using the `define()` function, which takes two arguments: the name of the constant, and its value. Here's an example of how to define a constant:

```
define("APP_NAME", "My PHP Application");
echo APP_NAME; // Output: My PHP Application
```

Note that the constant name must be written in uppercase letters, it's a common practice to use uppercase letters when naming constants.

Constants are typically used to store configuration settings or other values that will not change during the execution of the script, such as:

• Application name

• Version number

• Path to a file

• Database credentials

A variable is a storage location that can hold a value, which can be changed during the execution of the script. Variables are defined by prefixing their name with a dollar sign ($), and they can be used to store any type of data such as:

• Numbers (integers and floats)

• Strings

• Booleans

• Arrays

• Objects

• Resources

Here's an example of how to define a variable and assign a value to it:

```
$name = "John Doe";
$age = 30;
$isStudent = false;
```

In this example, we defined three variables `$name`, `$age`, `$isStudent` and assigned them values.

Keep in mind that variables don't have to be declared before they are used, and that the value of a variable can change throughout the script.

In summary, constants and variables are both used to store data in PHP, but constants are immutable and are typically used for values that will not change during the execution of the script, while variables are mutable and can be used to store any type of data that may change throughout the script.

Chapter 3: Operators and Control Structures

3.1 Operators

In PHP, operators are symbols or keywords that are used to perform operations on variables and values. PHP supports several types of operators, including:

○ **Arithmetic operators**: These operators are used to perform mathematical operations such as addition, subtraction, multiplication, division, and modulus.

• `+` is used for addition

• `-` is used for subtraction

• `*` is used for multiplication

• `/` is used for division

• `%` is used for modulus (returns the remainder of a division)

Example:
```
$a = 10;
$b = 5;
$sum = $a + $b;
$sub = $a - $b;
$mul = $a * $b;
$div = $a / $b;
$mod = $a % $b;v
```

○ **Comparison operators**: These operators are used to compare two values and return a boolean value indicating whether the comparison is true or false.

• `== ` is used for equality

• `!=` is used for inequality

• `>` is used for greater than

• `<` is used for less than

• `>=` is used for greater than or equal to

• `<=` is used for less than or equal to

Example:
```
$a = 10;
$b = 5;
$isEqual = ($a == $b);
```

```
$isNotEqual = ($a != $b);
$isGreater = ($a > $b);
$isLess = ($a < $b);
$isGreaterEqual = ($a >= $b);
$isLessEqual = ($a <= $b);
```

o **Logical operators**: These operators are used to combine multiple comparisons or evaluations and return a boolean value indicating whether the combination is true or false.

- `&&` is used for and

- `||` is used for or

- `!` is used for not

Example:
```
$isStudent = true;
$isSmart = false;
$result = ($isStudent && $isSmart); //false
$result = ($isStudent || $isSmart); //true
$result = !$isStudent; //false
```

o **Assignment operators**: These operators are used to assign a value to a variable. There are shorthand versions that allow you to perform an operation and assign the result to a variable in a single step.

- `=` is used for assignment

- `+=` is used for addition and assignment

- `-=` is used for subtraction and assignment

- `*=` is used for multiplication and assignment

- `/=` is used for division and assignment

- `%=` is used for modulus and assignment

Example:
```
$a = 10;
$a += 5;
$a -= 5;
$a *= 5;
$a /= 5;
$a %= 5;
```

○ **Ternary operator**: This operator is a shorthand version of an `if-else` statement, it is a shorthand way of writing a `if-else` statement, it's syntax is `condition ? result1 : result2`. It evaluates the condition and if it's true it returns `result1`, otherwise it returns `result2`.

You can use these operators in various combinations to perform complex operations and evaluations in your PHP scripts.

It's important to understand the operator precedence and associativity, which determines the order in which operations are performed when multiple operators are used in the same expression.

Examples:

```
$a = 10;
$b = 20;
$c = $a + $b; // $c = 30
$d = $a * $b; // $d = 200
$e = $a == $b; // $e = false
$f = $a != $b; // $f = true
```

In these examples, we used arithmetic operators to perform mathematical operations, comparison operators to evaluate equality, and logical operator to evaluate inequality.

In summary, operators are a fundamental part of PHP, they allow you to perform operations on variables and values, and to create complex evaluations and conditions in your scripts. Understanding the different types of operators available in PHP, their syntax, and their behavior is essential to creating effective and efficient PHP scripts.

3.2 Control Structures

In PHP, control structures are used to control the flow of execution of a script. They allow you to create conditions and make decisions based on the results of those conditions. The most common control structures in PHP are:

• **if-else**: This control structure is used to execute a block of code if a certain condition is true, and another block of code if the condition is false. Here's an example of how to use an if-else statement:

```
$age = 25;
if ($age >= 21) {
    echo "Welcome to the party!";
```

```
} else {
    echo "Sorry, you're not old enough.";
}
```

• **if-elseif-else**: This control structure is used when you want to check multiple conditions and execute a different block of code for each condition. Here's an example of how to use an if-elseif-else statement:

```
$age = 25;
if ($age < 21) {
    echo "Sorry, you're not old enough.";
} elseif ($age >= 21 && $age < 30) {
    echo "Welcome to the party!";
} else {
    echo "You're a little too old for this party.";
}
```

• **switch**: This control structure is used when you want to check multiple conditions and execute a different block of code for each condition, but it's more appropriate when you're checking for multiple possible values of a variable. Here's an example of how to use a switch statement:

```
$day = "Sunday";

switch ($day) {
    case "Monday":
        echo "It's Monday, time to work.";
        break;
    case "Wednesday":
        echo "It's Wednesday, keep pushing.";
        break;
    case "Friday":
        echo "It's Friday, time to party!";
        break;
    case "Sunday":
        echo "It's Sunday, time to spend with family and
friends.";
        break;
    default:
        echo "It's just another day.";
}
```

• **while and do-while loops**: These control structures are used to execute a block of code multiple times while a certain condition is true. The while loop checks the condition before executing the code, and the do-while loop checks the condition after executing the code. Here's an example of how to use a while loop:

```
$i = 1;
while ($i <= 10) {
    echo $i . " ";
    $i++;
}
```

The loop will repeat until the condition `$i <= 10` is false, at that point the loop will be terminated and the script execution continues.

It's important to note that if the condition in while loop never becomes false, it will cause an infinite loop, this can cause problems such as freezing or crashing the script, or even stopping the execution of the script.

And here's an example of how to use a do-while loop:

```
$i = 1;
do {
    echo $i . " ";
    $i++;
} while ($i <= 10);
```

In this example the do-while loop will execute 10 times and will print numbers from 1 to 10 with a space after each number.

• **for loops**: This control structure is used to execute a block of code a specific number of times. It's often used when you know exactly how many times you want to iterate.

Here's an example of how to use a for loop:

```
for ($i = 1; $i <= 10; $i++) {
    echo $i . " ";
}
```

In the example above, the for loop initializes the variable `$i` to 1, then checks if `$i` is less than or equal to 10, and if so, it executes the block of code inside the loop, and finally increments `$i` by 1.

The loop continues to execute as long as the condition is true.

Here's an example of a more complex **for** loop:

```php
$items = array("item1", "item2", "item3", "item4", "item5");

for ($i = 0; $i < count($items); $i++) {
    if ($i % 2 == 0) {
        echo $items[$i] . " is even.\n";
    } else {
        echo $items[$i] . " is odd.\n";
    }
}
```

In this example, we have an array `$items` containing 5 elements. The for loop starts with the keyword `for`, followed by the initialization of the variable `$i` with the value of 0, then the condition `$i < count($items)` and the increment `$i++`.

Inside the loop, there are two `echo` statements: one for the even elements, and the other for the odd elements. The if-else statement is used to check if the current element is even or odd. If the remainder of the division of `$i` by 2 is equal to 0, it means that the current element is even, otherwise it's odd.

So, in this example the for loop will iterate through all the elements of the `$items` array and will print if the element is odd or even with the corresponding value of the element.

It's important to note that this is a complex example that uses different concepts such as arrays, if-else and the modulus operator, but it demonstrates how you can use a for loop in a more advanced way to perform different operations on the elements of an array.

In summary, control structures are an essential part of PHP programming, they allow you to control the flow of execution of your script, create conditions and make decisions based on the results of those conditions.

Understanding how to use control structures such as if-else, switch, while, do-while and for loops is essential for creating effective and efficient PHP scripts.

Chapter 4: Functions

4.1 Introduction to Function

A function is a block of code that performs a specific task and can be called multiple times throughout a script. Functions in PHP are used to organize and reuse code, making it more maintainable and efficient.

The purpose of a function is to encapsulate a specific task or a set of instructions, so that it can be called by other parts of the script, without having to repeat the same code multiple times. This helps to avoid code duplication and improve readability. Functions also provide a way to divide a complex task into smaller, manageable pieces.

Functions are defined using the `function` keyword, followed by a unique name, and a set of instructions inside a pair of curly braces `{}`. Once a function is defined, it can be called by using its name followed by a pair of parentheses `()`. Functions can also accept parameters, which are values passed to the function when it's called, and they can return a value back to the calling code.

In PHP, there are two types of functions: built-in functions, which are functions that are already available in PHP, and user-defined functions, which are created by the developer. The built-in functions provide a wide range of functionality, such as string manipulation, file system operations, and mathematical calculations.

It's important to note that when you're using functions in your code, it's essential to give them meaningful and descriptive names, so that it's easy to understand what the function does just by reading its name. Also, it's a good practice to document your functions using comments, describing what the function does, the parameters it takes, and the values it returns.

Using functions in your PHP code can make it more organized, readable, and maintainable, and it can also help you to avoid duplication of code. As you learn more about functions and their capabilities, you'll be able to create more complex and powerful scripts, so understanding functions is an important step to mastering PHP programming.

4.2 Defining and Calling Functions

In PHP, functions are defined using the function keyword, followed by a unique name, and a set of instructions inside a pair of curly braces `{}`. The name of the function should be descriptive and meaningful, it should indicate what the function does.

Here's an example of a simple function that takes no parameters and returns no values:

```
function sayHello() {
    echo "Hello World!";
}
```

In this example, we have defined a function called `sayHello()`, which simply displays the message "Hello World!" when it's called.

To call a function, you simply use its name followed by a pair of parentheses `()`. Here's an example of how to call the `sayHello()` function:

```
sayHello();
```

This will execute the code inside the function, which in this case will display "Hello World!" on the screen.

Functions can also accept parameters, which are values passed to the function when it's called. Here's an example of a function that takes two parameters:

```
function addNumbers($a, $b) {
    $sum = $a + $b;
    echo "The sum of $a and $b is $sum.";
}
```

In this example, we have defined a function called `addNumbers()`, which takes two parameters called `$a` and `$b`. When this function is called, it will add the two numbers together, and display the result on the screen.

Here's an example of how to call the `addNumbers()` function and pass it two parameters:

```
addNumbers(5, 10);
```

This will execute the code inside the function and display the message "The sum of 5 and 10 is 15."

Functions can also return a value back to the calling code, using the return keyword. Here 's an example of a function that takes two parameters and returns their sum:

```
function add($a, $b) {
    return $a + $b;
}
```

In this example, we have defined a function called `add()`, which takes two parameters `$a` and `$b`, and returns their sum using the `return` keyword.

Here's an example of how to call the `add()` function and use its returned value:

```
$result = add(5, 10);
echo "The sum of 5 and 10 is $result.";
```

This will execute the function and assign the returned value to the variable `$result`, and then display the message "The sum of 5 and 10 is 15."

When you're defining functions, it's important to keep in mind that the names of the parameters must be unique within the function, and they can't have the same name as a global variable.

4.3 Function Scope and Global Variables

In PHP, the scope of a variable refers to the parts of the script where the variable can be accessed or used. Variables defined within a function have a local scope, which means they can only be accessed within the function where they are defined. Variables defined outside of a function have a global scope, which means they can be accessed from anywhere within the script.

For example, consider the following code:

```
$x = 5;

function addTwo() {
    $x = $x + 2;
    echo $x;
}

addTwo();
```

In this example, the variable `$x` is defined outside of the function `addTwo()`, and it is given a value of `5`. Inside the function, a new local variable `$x` is created and its value is set to `$x + 2`, this should throw an error because the variable inside the function is not aware of the global variable, and it's trying to use a variable that is not defined yet.

To make the function aware of the `global` variable and make it able to modify it, you have to use the keyword global before the variable inside the function.

```
$x = 5;

function addTwo() {
    global $x;
    $x = $x + 2;
    echo $x;
}

addTwo();
```

In this case, the function is now able to access and modify the global variable `$x`, and the code will output `7`.

It's important to keep in mind that global variables should be used sparingly, as they can make the code harder to understand and maintain. It's generally considered a better practice to pass values to a function as arguments and return values as needed, rather than relying on global variables.

4.4 Recursion and Recursive Functions

Recursion is a technique in which a function calls itself, either directly or indirectly. A function that calls itself is called a recursive function. Recursion can be a powerful tool for solving problems, as it allows you to break down a complex task into smaller, simpler sub-tasks that can be solved using the same function.

A recursive function must have a base case, which is a condition that stops the recursion. Without a base case, the function would keep calling itself indefinitely, resulting in a stack overflow error.

Here's an example of a recursive function that calculates the factorial of a number:

```
function factorial($n) {
    if ($n == 0) {
        return 1;
    }
    return $n * factorial($n - 1);
}
```

In this example, the function `factorial()` takes an argument `$n`, and it calls itself with the argument `$n - 1` until the base case `$n == 0` is reached. The base case returns the value `1`, and each recursive call multiplies its argument by the result of the previous call.

Here's an example of how to call the `factorial()` function:

```
$result = factorial(5);
echo "The factorial of 5 is $result.";
```

This will call the function with the argument `5`, and it will output "The factorial of 5 is 120."

Recursive functions can be used to solve a wide range of problems, such as traversing a tree data structure, solving mathematical problems, or generating permutations and combinations.

It's important to keep in mind that recursion requires a significant amount of memory, and it can also lead to a stack overflow error if the base case is not defined properly or if the recursive calls are too deep. It's generally considered a better practice to use an iterative approach instead of recursion when it's possible.

4.5 Anonymous Functions and Closures

In PHP, an anonymous function is a function without a name. Anonymous functions are also known as closures and they are created using the `function` keyword followed by a set of instructions inside a pair of curly braces `{}`. Anonymous functions can be used as arguments or return values, which makes them a powerful tool for creating small, reusable blocks of code.

Here's an example of an anonymous function that takes a single argument and returns its square:

```
$square = function($x) {
    return $x * $x;
};
```

In this example, the anonymous function is assigned to the variable `$square`, and it can be called just like any other function:

```
$result = $square(5);
echo "The square of 5 is $result.";
```

This will output "The square of 5 is 25."

Another example of when anonymous functions are used is when they are passed as an argument to a function. For example, the `array_map` function takes two arguments: an array and a callback function. The callback function is applied to each element of the array and returns a new array.

```php
$numbers = [1, 2, 3, 4, 5];
$squaredNumbers = array_map(function($x) {
    return $x * $x;
}, $numbers);
```

In this example, `array_map` applies the anonymous function to each element of the array `$numbers`, and it returns a new array of squared numbers.

Closures are anonymous functions that have access to the variables defined in the outer scope even after the outer function has returned. This is achieved by binding the closure to the variables it needs from the outer scope.

```php
$age = 25;
$myAge = function() use ($age) {
    return $age;
};
```

In this example, the closure is bound to the variable `$age` from the outer scope, so it can still access its value even after the outer function has returned.

It's important to keep in mind that anonymous functions are only available in PHP version 5.3 or later. And also that when using closures, it's important to be aware of any variables from the outer scope that the closure uses, as they may change in unexpected ways and cause bugs in your code.

In summary, Anonymous functions and closures are a powerful way to create and use small, reusable blocks of code in PHP. They can be used to improve the readability and maintainability of your code, and also to make it more flexible and efficient. As you continue to learn and develop your skills with PHP, you'll likely find many other ways to use these powerful constructs.

4.6 Built-in Functions

PHP provides a wide range of built-in functions that can be used to perform various tasks, such as string manipulation, array manipulation, and file system operations. In this subchapter, we'll take a look at some of the most commonly used built-in functions in PHP.

○ String Manipulation Functions:

PHP provides a variety of string manipulation functions, such as `strlen()`, `substr()`, `str_replace()`, and `strpos()`. These functions can be used to perform common tasks such as counting the number of characters in a string, extracting a portion of a string, replacing a specific part of a string, or finding the position of a specific substring within a string.

- `strlen()`: This function returns the length of a string. It takes a single argument, which is the string to be measured.

```
$string = "Hello World!";
$length = strlen($string);
echo "The length of the string is $length";
```

This will output "The length of the string is 12".

- `substr()`: This function returns a portion of a string. It takes three arguments: the string to extract from, the starting position, and the number of characters to extract.

```
$string = "Hello World!";
$substring = substr($string, 6, 5);
echo "The substring is $substring";
```

This will output "The substring is World"

- `str_replace()`: This function replaces all occurrences of a search string with a replacement string. It takes three arguments: the search string, the replacement string, and the original string.

```
$string = "Hello World!";
$newstring = str_replace("World", "PHP", $string);
echo $newstring;
```

This will output "Hello PHP!"

- `strpos()`: This function finds the position of the first occurrence of a substring in a string. It takes two arguments: the substring to search for, and the original string.

```
$string = "Hello World!";
$position = strpos($string, "World");
echo "The position of the substring is $position";
```

This will output "The position of the substring is 6".

These are some of the most common string manipulation functions in PHP, and they can be used to perform a wide range of tasks such as counting characters, extracting substrings, and replacing or finding specific parts of a string.

○ **Array Functions:**

PHP also provides a variety of array manipulation functions such as `count()`, `sort()`, `array_search()`, and `array_merge()`. These functions can be used to perform common tasks such as counting the number of elements in an array, sorting an array, searching for a specific value in an array, or merging two or more arrays.

• `count()`: This function returns the number of elements in an array. It takes a single argument, which is the array to be counted.

```
$numbers = [1, 2, 3, 4, 5];
$count = count($numbers);
echo "The array has $count elements.";
```

This will output "The array has 5 elements."

• `sort()`: This function sorts the elements of an array in ascending order. It takes a single argument, which is the array to be sorted.

```
$numbers = [5, 2, 1, 4, 3];
sort($numbers);
print_r($numbers);
```

This will output `Array ( [0] => 1 [1] => 2 [2] => 3 [3] => 4 [4] => 5 )`

• `array_search()`: This function searches for a value in an array and returns the key of the first matching element. It takes two arguments: the value to search for and the array to search in.

```
$numbers = [1, 2, 3, 4, 5];
$key = array_search(3, $numbers);
echo "The key of the value is $key";
```

This will output "The key of the value is 2"

• `array_merge()`: This function merges two or more arrays. It takes any number of arrays as arguments and returns a new array that contains all the elements of the input arrays.

```
$numbers1 = [1, 2, 3];
$numbers2 = [4, 5, 6];
$numbers3 = [7, 8, 9];
$merged_numbers = array_merge($numbers1, $numbers2, $numbers3);
print_r($merged_numbers);
```

This will output Array ([0] => 1 [1] => 2 [2] => 3 [3] => 4 [4] => 5 [5] => 6 [6] => 7 [7] => 8 [8] => 9)

These are some of the most common array manipulation functions in PHP, and they can be used to perform a wide range of tasks such as counting elements, sorting arrays, searching for specific values and merging arrays.

○ **File System Functions:**

PHP also provides a variety of file system functions such as `fopen()`, `fread()`, `fwrite()`, and `fclose()`. These functions can be used to perform common tasks such as opening, reading, writing, and closing a file.

• `fopen()`: This function is used to open a file. It takes two parameters: the name of the file and the mode in which the file is to be opened. The mode can be "r" for reading, "w" for writing, "a" for appending, and "x" for creating and opening a new file for writing.

```
$file = fopen("example.txt", "r");
```

This opens a file called "example.txt" in "read" mode and assigns the file pointer to the variable `$file`.

• `fread()`: This function is used to read a block of data from a file. It takes two parameters: a file pointer to the file to be read and the number of bytes to be read. It returns the read data as a string.be "r" for reading, "w" for writing, "a" for appending, and "x" for creating and opening a new file for writing.

```
$content = fread($file, filesize("example.txt"));
```

This reads the contents of the file that the file pointer "$file" is pointing to, and stores it in the "$content" variable. The first argument is the file pointer and the second argument is the size of the file, in this case is obtained using the filesize function.

• `fwrite()`: This function is used to write data to a file. It takes two parameters: a file pointer to the file to be written to and the data to be written. It returns the number of bytes written to the file and it returns the read data as a string.be "r" for reading, "w" for writing, "a" for appending, and "x" for creating and opening a new file for writing.

```
fwrite($file, "Hello, World!");
```

This writes the string "Hello, World!" to the file that the file pointer "$file" is pointing to. The first argument is the file pointer and the second argument is the data to be written.

- `fclose()`: This function is used to close a file. It takes a single parameter, which is a file pointer to the file that is to be closed.

```
fclose($file);
```

This closes the file that the file pointer "$file" is pointing to.

It's important to notice that when working with files, you should always close the file after you are done with it, as this will free up resources and prevent data corruption. Also, you should always check the return value of the `fopen()` function to make sure that the file was opened successfully before attempting to read or write to it.

4.7 Advanced Function Concepts

○ Variable-Length Argument Lists

In PHP 7.0 and later versions, you can use the `...` operator (also known as the splat operator) to create a variable-length argument list in a function. This allows you to accept an unknown number of arguments and access them through an array. For example:

```
function addNumbers(...$args) {
  $sum = 0;
  foreach ($args as $arg) {
    $sum += $arg;
  }
  return $sum;
}

echo addNumbers(1, 2, 3, 4); // Output: 10
```

In this example, the `...$args` syntax creates an array called `$args` that contains all of the arguments passed to the `addNumbers()` function.

○ Callbacks

In addition to passing a callback function to built-in functions such as `array_map()` and `array_filter()`, you can also create your own functions that take a callback as an argument.

For example, you could create a `processArray()` function that takes an array and a callback function as arguments, and then applies the callback to each element of the array:

```php
function processArray(array $arr, callable $callback) {
    return array_map($callback, $arr);
}

$numbers = [1, 2, 3, 4];
$doubled_numbers = processArray($numbers, function($n) { return $n
* 2; });
print_r($doubled_numbers); // Output: Array ( [0] => 2 [1] => 4
[2] => 6 [3] => 8 )
```

You can also use the `call_user_func()` and `call_user_func_array()` functions to call a callback function with a specified set of arguments. For example:

```php
function add($a, $b) {
    return $a + $b;
}

$result = call_user_func('add', 1, 2);
echo $result; // Output: 3

$result = call_user_func_array('add', [1, 2]);
echo $result; // Output: 3
```

○ **Type Hinting**

Type hinting is a way to specify the type of a parameter in a function. This helps to ensure that the correct type of argument is passed to the function and can also make your code more readable. For example, you can use type hinting to specify that a parameter should be a callable:

```php
function processNumber(int $n, callable $callback) {
    return $callback($n);
}

$result = processNumber(5, function($n) { return $n * 2; });
echo $result; // Output: 10
```

You can also use self and parent type hints to specify that a parameter should be of the same class or a parent class of the class where the function is defined.

Chapter 5: Arrays

5.1 Introduction to Arrays

Arrays are a fundamental data structure in PHP and are used to store and organize multiple values into a single variable. They are similar to lists or collections in other programming languages. In PHP, arrays can store a variety of data types, including integers, strings, and objects.

○ Declaring and Initializing Arrays

Arrays can be declared using the `array` keyword or by using square brackets `[]`. For example:

```
$numbers = array(1, 2, 3, 4);
$names = ["Alice", "Bob", "Charlie"];
```

You can also initialize an array with no values by simply declaring it:

```
$empty_array = array();
$empty_array2 = [];
```

○ Accessing Array Elements

Array elements can be accessed by using the array name followed by the index of the element in square brackets. The index of the first element in an array is 0, and the index of the last element is the size of the array minus one. For example:

```
$names = ["Alice", "Bob", "Charlie"];
echo $names[1]; // Output: "Bob"
```

You can also use the `var_dump()` function to display the contents of an array and its data types.

```
$mixed_array = [1, "hello", true, [1,2,3]];
var_dump($mixed_array);
```

○ Array Operations

You can use various array functions in PHP to manipulate arrays, such as:

• count(): Returns the number of elements in an array

• sort(): Sorts the elements of an array in ascending order

• rsort(): Sorts the elements of an array in descending order

- `implode()`: Join array elements with a string

- `explode()`: Split a string into an array

For example:
```
$numbers = [2, 3, 1, 4];
sort($numbers);
print_r($numbers); // Output: Array ( [0] => 1 [1] => 2 [2] => 3
[3] => 4 )
```

5.2 Manipulating Arrays

Manipulating arrays is a common task in PHP, and there are many built-in functions and techniques that can be used to do so. In this subchapter, we'll cover some of the most commonly used array functions and techniques for sorting, filtering, and merging arrays.

○ **Sorting Arrays**

There are several built-in functions in PHP for sorting arrays, including `sort()`, `rsort()`, `asort()`, and `arsort()`.

- `sort()`: Sorts the elements of an array in ascending order, according to their values.
```
$fruits = array("lemon", "orange", "banana", "apple");
sort($fruits);
print_r($fruits); // Output: Array ( [0] => apple [1] => banana
[2] => lemon [3] => orange )
```

- `rsort()`: Sorts the elements of an array in descending order, according to their values.
```
$numbers = [2, 3, 1, 4];
rsort($numbers);
print_r($numbers); // Output: Array ( [0] => 4 [1] => 3 [2] => 2
[3] => 1 )
```

- `asort()`: Sorts the elements of an array in ascending order, according to their values, and preserves the key-value associations.
```
$associative_array = array("a" => "apple", "b" => "banana", "c" =>
"cherry");
asort($associative_array);
print_r($associative_array);
// Output: Array ( [b] => banana [a] => apple [c] => cherry )
```

• arsort(): Sorts the elements of an array in descending order, according to their values, and preserves the key-value associations.

```
$associative_array = array("a" => "apple", "b" => "banana", "c" =>
"cherry");
arsort($associative_array);
print_r($associative_array);
/* Output:
Array ( [c] => cherry [a] => apple [b] => banana )
*/
```

○ **Filtering Arrays**

You can use the `array_filter()` function to filter out elements in an array based on a certain condition. For example:

```
$numbers = [1, 2, 3, 4, 5];
$even_numbers = array_filter($numbers, function ($number) {
    return $number % 2 == 0;
});
print_r($even_numbers); // Output: Array ( [1] => 2 [3] => 4 )
```

○ **Merging Arrays**

You can use the `array_merge()` function to merge two or more arrays together. For example:

```
$numbers1 = [1, 2, 3];
$numbers2 = [4, 5, 6];
$numbers3 = [7, 8, 9];
$merged_numbers = array_merge($numbers1, $numbers2, $numbers3);
print_r($merged_numbers); // Output: Array ( [0] => 1 [1] => 2 [2]
=> 3 [3] => 4 [4] => 5 [5] => 6 [6] => 7 [7] => 8 [8] => 9 )
```

When merging arrays, it's important to keep in mind that if multiple arrays have elements with the same key, the last value with that key will overwrite any previous values.

```
$array1 = array("color" => "red", 2, 4);
$array2 = array("a", "color" => "green", "b", "shape" => "trape-
zoid", 4);
$result = array_merge($array1, $array2);
print_r($result);
/* Output:
```

```
Array
(
    [color] => green
    [0] => 2
    [1] => 4
    [2] => a
    [3] => b
    [shape] => trapezoid
    [4] => 4
)
*/
```

You can also use the `+` operator to merge arrays:

```
$array1 = array("color" => "red", 2, 4);
$array2 = array("a", "color" => "green", "b", "shape" => "trape-
zoid", 4);
$result = $array1 + $array2;
print_r($result);
/* Output:
Array
(
    [color] => red
    [0] => 2
    [1] => 4
    [2] => a
    [3] => b
    [shape] => trapezoid
    [4] => 4
)
*/
```

As you can see, the `+` operator does not overwrite the value of the same key like `array_merge()` does.

Another example is using `array_push` to merge an array into another array:

```
$colors1 = array("red", "green", "blue");
$colors2 = array("purple", "yellow", "orange");
foreach($colors2 as $val) {
    array_push($colors1, $val);
}
print_r($colors1);
// Output: Array ( [0] => red [1] => green [2] => blue [3] => pur-
ple [4] => yellow [5] => orange )
```

Or also you can use the `...` operator to merge multiple arrays:

```
$colors1 = array("red", "green", "blue");
$colors2 = array("purple", "yellow");
$colors3 = array("orange");
$colors = [...$colors1,...$colors2,...$colors3];
print_r($colors);
// Output: Array ( [0] => red [1] => green [2] => blue [3] => pur-
ple [4] => yellow [5] => orange )
```

You can also use the `array_combine()` function to create a new array by using one array for keys and another for its values:

```
$keys = array("a", "b", "c");
$values = array("red", "green", "blue");
$colors = array_combine($keys, $values);
print_r($colors);
// Output: Array ( [a] => red [b] => green [c] => blue )
```

There are many ways to merge arrays in PHP, these are just a few examples. Each method has its own use cases and should be chosen based on the specific requirements of your application.

5.3 Multi-dimensional Arrays

In PHP, an array can contain other arrays, known as multi-dimensional arrays. These arrays can be useful for organizing and manipulating data in more complex ways. In this subchapter, we will cover how to create, navigate, and manipulate multi-dimensional arrays.

○ **Creating Multi-dimensional Arrays**

There are several ways to create a multi-dimensional array in PHP. One way is to use nested square brackets, like so:

```
$colors = array(
    array("red", "green", "blue"),
    array("purple", "yellow", "orange"),
    array("pink", "gray", "black")
);
```

Another way is to use the `array()` function with multiple levels of nested arrays:

```
$colors = array(
    "primary" => array("red", "green", "blue"),
```

```
    "secondary" => array("purple", "yellow", "orange"),
    "tertiary" => array("pink", "gray", "black")
);
```

You can also use the `[]` operator to create an empty array and then add elements to it:

```
$colors = [];
$colors[] = ["red", "green", "blue"];
$colors[] = ["purple", "yellow", "orange"];
$colors[] = ["pink", "gray", "black"];
```

○ **Navigating Multi-dimensional Arrays**

Once a multi-dimensional array has been created, it can be accessed by using multiple levels of array notation. For example, to access the "green" element in the first array of the `$colors` array, you would use the following code:

```
echo $colors[0][1]; // Output: green
```

You can also use the foreach loop to navigate through a multi-dimensional array:

```
foreach ($fruits as $group => $items) {
    echo $group . ":<br>";
    foreach ($items as $item) {
        echo "- " . $item . "<br>";
    }
}
```

This code would output:

```
citrus:
- orange
- lemon
- lime
berries:
- strawberry
- raspberry
- blackberry
apples:
- red delicious
- granny smith
```

○ Manipulating Multi-dimensional Arrays

There are many built-in functions and techniques that can be used to manipulate multi-dimensional arrays. For example, the `array_walk_recursive()` function can be used to apply a user-defined function to every element of a multi-dimensional array:

```php
function add_star(&$value, $key) {
    $value .= "*";
}
array_walk_recursive($colors, "add_star");
```

You can also use the `array_column()` function to extract a single column from a multi-dimensional array:

```php
$colors_primary = array_column($colors, 0);
```

Finally, you can use the `array_map()` function to apply a callback function to all elements of an array:

```php
$colors_uppercase = array_map(function($color_set) {
    return array_map('strtoupper', $color_set);
}, $colors);
```

It's important to note that manipulating multi-dimensional arrays can become complex quickly and you should be careful when using these functions and when navigating multi-dimensional arrays.

5.4 Array Iteration

Array iteration is a common task in PHP programming and there are several ways to loop through arrays, including `foreach`, `for`, and `while` loops. Let's go through each method in detail.

○ Foreach Loop

The `foreach` loop is specifically designed to iterate through arrays. It allows you to loop through each element in the array and perform some action on each element. Here is an example of using a `foreach` loop to print each element in an array:

```php
$fruits = array("apple", "banana", "cherry");
foreach ($fruits as $fruit) {
    echo $fruit . "<br>";
}
```

This code would output:

```
apple
banana
cherry
```

The `foreach` loop has two parts: the loop expression and the loop body. The loop expression consists of the keyword "foreach", followed by the array to iterate over in parentheses, and then the as keyword followed by the variable that will hold the current value of the iteration. The loop body contains the code that will be executed for each iteration of the loop.

○ **For Loop**

The `for` loop is a general-purpose loop that can be used to iterate through arrays. To use a `for` loop with an array, you need to use the array length function "count" to determine the number of elements in the array and use a counter variable to keep track of the current iteration. Here is an example of using a `for` loop to print each element in an array:

```
$fruits = array("apple", "banana", "cherry");

for ($i = 0; $i < count($fruits); $i++) {
    echo $fruits[$i] . "<br>";
}
```

This code would output:

```
apple
banana
cherry
```

○ **While Loop**

The `while` loop is a general-purpose loop that can be used to iterate through arrays. To use a `while` loop with an array, you need to use a counter variable to keep track of the current iteration and use a conditional statement to determine when to stop looping. Here is an example of using a `while` loop to print each element in an array:

```
$fruits = array("apple", "banana", "cherry");
$i = 0;
while ($i < count($fruits)) {
    echo $fruits[$i] . "<br>";
    $i++;
}
```

This code would output the same result as the `foreach` and `for` loop.

It's important to understand the differences between these looping methods and choose the one that best fits your needs for each particular situation. The `foreach` loop is the simplest and most straightforward way to loop through arrays, but the `for` and `while` loops offer more control and flexibility in certain situations.

5.5 Array and Object Interaction

Arrays and objects are two fundamental data structures in PHP, and understanding how they interact with each other is important for developing efficient and scalable applications. This subchapter will cover the conversion of arrays to objects and objects to arrays, as well as the use of arrays and objects together.

○ **Converting Arrays to Objects**

Arrays can be converted to objects in PHP by using the type casting syntax. This allows you to create an object with properties and values defined by the elements in an array. For example:

```
$array = array("first_name" => "John", "last_name" => "Doe");
$object = (object) $array;

echo $object->first_name; // Output: John
echo $object->last_name; // Output: Doe
```

○ **Converting Objects to Arrays**

Similarly, objects can be converted to arrays in PHP. This is useful when you need to manipulate or sort the data stored in an object. To convert an object to an array, you can use the `get_object_vars()` function. For example:

```
$object = new stdClass();
$object->first_name = "John";
$object->last_name = "Doe";

$array = (array) $object;

print_r($array);
/* Output:
Array
(
    [first_name] => John
    [last_name] => Doe
)*/
```

○ Using Arrays and Objects Together

Arrays and objects can be used together in PHP to provide a flexible and dynamic data structure. For example, you can create an array of objects, where each object represents a record in a database. To access the data stored in each object, you can use the array notation or object notation, depending on your preference and the requirements of your application. For example:

```php
$records = array();

$record1 = new stdClass();
$record1->first_name = "John";
$record1->last_name = "Doe";

$record2 = new stdClass();
$record2->first_name = "Jane";
$record2->last_name = "Doe";

$records[] = $record1;
$records[] = $record2;

foreach ($records as $record) {
    echo $record->first_name . " " . $record->last_name . "<br>";
}
/* Output:
John Doe
Jane Doe
*/
```

Arrays and objects are versatile data structures in PHP, and understanding their interaction can greatly enhance your ability to develop effective and efficient applications.

5.6 Array Performance

Arrays are a crucial data structure in PHP and their performance can greatly impact the overall performance of your code. It is essential to understand the performance characteristics of the different types of arrays in PHP and choose the right type of array for a given task.

In PHP, there are three main types of arrays: `indexed arrays`, `associative arrays`, and `multidimensional` arrays. Each type of array has different performance characteristics that make them more or less suitable for different use cases.

○ Indexed Arrays

Indexed arrays are the simplest type of array in PHP and are optimized for fast access to elements. They are implemented as contiguous blocks of memory, which makes accessing elements by index number very fast. To declare an indexed array, simply use square brackets to enclose a list of comma-separated values:

```php
$fruits = ['apple', 'banana', 'cherry'];
```

Indexed arrays have a fast O(1) time complexity for accessing and inserting elements, making them ideal for tasks such as iterating through a large number of elements:

```php
for ($i = 0; $i < count($fruits); $i++) {
    echo $fruits[$i] . "\n";
}
```

○ Associative Arrays

Associative arrays are similar to indexed arrays, but the elements are accessed by keys instead of indices. They are slower than indexed arrays for accessing and inserting elements because the keys must be searched for, but they are much more flexible and can be used in situations where the size of the array is not known in advance.

```php
$fruits = [
    'red' => 'apple',
    'yellow' => 'banana',
    'dark_red' => 'cherry'
];
```

Associative arrays are ideal for tasks such as looking up values by key:

```php
echo $fruits['red']; // Outputs: apple
```

○ Multidimensional Arrays

Multidimensional arrays are arrays that contain arrays. They can be used to represent complex data structures, but they are slower to access and manipulate than either indexed or associative arrays.

```php
$fruits = [
    ['apple', 'red'],
    ['banana', 'yellow'],
```

```
    ['cherry', 'dark_red']
];
```

Multidimensional arrays are best used sparingly and only when the added complexity is necessary. To access elements in a multidimensional array, you can use multiple square brackets:

```
echo $fruits[0][0]; // Outputs: apple
```

○ Choosing the Right Array Type

When choosing the right type of array for a given task, it's important to consider the size of the array, the type of operations you'll be performing, and the data structure you're trying to represent.

For large arrays with a lot of operations, indexed arrays are often the best choice due to their fast $O(1)$ access and insertion time complexity.

For small arrays with complex operations, associative arrays may be a better choice because they are more flexible and allow you to access elements by key.

For complex data structures, multidimensional arrays may be necessary. However, keep in mind that they are slower to access and manipulate than either indexed or associative arrays.

In conclusion, by understanding the performance characteristics of the different types of arrays.

5.7 Advanced Array Concepts

In this subchapter, we will cover advanced array concepts such as closures, recursion, and Iterators. These topics are essential for advanced PHP programming and will give you a deeper understanding of how arrays can be used in PHP.

○ Closures in Arrays

Closures are anonymous functions that can be stored in variables and passed as arguments to other functions. In PHP, closures can be used in arrays to define complex operations on the array elements. For example, you can use a closure to sort an array of numbers in ascending or descending order:

```
$numbers = [3, 1, 4, 1, 5, 9, 2, 6, 5, 3, 5];
// sort the array in ascending order
```

```php
usort($numbers, function ($a, $b) {
    return $a - $b;
});

print_r($numbers);
// Output: Array ( [0] => 1 [1] => 1 [2] => 2 [3] => 3 [4] => 3
[5] => 4 [6] => 5 [7] => 5 [8] => 5 [9] => 6 [10] => 9 )

// sort the array in descending order
usort($numbers, function ($a, $b) {
    return $b - $a;
});

print_r($numbers);
// Output: Array ( [0] => 9 [1] => 6 [2] => 5 [3] => 5 [4] => 5
[5] => 4 [6] => 3 [7] => 3 [8] => 2 [9] => 1 [10] => 1 )
```

○ **Recursion in Arrays**

Recursion is a technique where a function calls itself to solve a problem. In PHP, recursion can be used to traverse complex arrays and perform operations on their elements. For example, you can use recursion to find the sum of all elements in a multi-dimensional array:

```php
$numbers = [1, 2, [3, 4, [5, 6]], 7, 8];

function sumArray($array) {
    $sum = 0;
    foreach ($array as $value) {
        if (is_array($value)) {
            $sum += sumArray($value);
        } else {
            $sum += $value;
        }
    }
    return $sum;
}
echo sumArray($numbers);
// Output: 36
```

○ **Iterators in Arrays**

Iterators are objects that allow you to traverse arrays in a simple and efficient way. PHP provides several built-in iterators, such as `ArrayIterator` and

`RecursiveArrayIterator`, that can be used to loop through arrays and perform operations on their elements. For example, you can use `ArrayIterator` to sort an array and print its elements:

```php
$numbers = [3, 1, 4, 1, 5, 9, 2, 6, 5, 3, 5];

$iterator = new ArrayIterator($numbers);
sort($iterator);

foreach ($iterator as $value) {
    echo $value . ' ';
}
// Output: 1 1 2 3 3 4 5 5 5 6 9
```

In conclusion, these advanced array concepts will help you to write more efficient and sophisticated code in PHP. Understanding closures, recursion, and iterators is a key step towards becoming a proficient.

Chapter 6: Object-Oriented Programming

6.1 Understanding Classes and Objects

Classes and objects are fundamental concepts in object-oriented programming. In PHP, classes are used to define objects that have properties and methods. Objects are instances of classes and have unique values for their properties.

Classes and objects provide a way to structure and organize your code, making it more readable, maintainable, and reusable. They also allow you to encapsulate data and behavior within a single unit, making your code more secure and preventing unwanted access to your data.

Here's a simple example of how you can define a class in PHP:

```php
class Car {
  public $make;
  public $model;
  public $year;

  public function honk() {
    return "Beep beep!";
  }
}
```

In this example, we have defined a class called Car with three properties: `$make`, `$model`, and `$year`. The class also has a method called honk that returns a string. To create an object from this class, you would use the following syntax:

```php
$myCar = new Car();
$myCar->make = "Toyota";
$myCar->model = "Camry";
$myCar->year = 2020;

echo $myCar->honk(); // outputs "Beep beep!"
```

In this example, we created an object called `$myCar` and assigned values to its properties. We also called the `honk` method on the object and output the result.

By using classes and objects, you can build complex applications with a clear structure and hierarchy. In the following subchapters, we'll dive deeper into class properties and methods, constructors and destructors, inheritance and polymorphism, and the scope resolution operator.

6.2 Defining class Properties and Methods

Classes in PHP allow us to encapsulate data and behavior into reusable, self-contained entities. In this subchapter, we will cover how to define properties and methods within a class.

Properties are the data members of a class, which store the state of an object. They are defined by using the keyword `var` followed by the property name. For example:

```php
$myCar = new Car();
$myCar->make = "Toyota";
$myCar->model = "Camry";
$myCar->year = 2020;

echo $myCar->honk(); // outputs "Beep beep!"
```

Methods are the behavior of a class, which define the actions that can be performed by objects of that class. They are defined using the keyword `function`, followed by the method name. For example:

```php
class Car {
  var $make;
  var $model;
  var $year;

  function startEngine() {
    return "The engine has started.";
  }
}
```

By convention, method names are written in CamelCase, starting with a verb that describes the action performed by the method.

We can access the properties and methods of an object using the `->` operator. For example:

```php
$myCar = new Car();
$myCar->make = "Toyota";
$myCar->model = "Camry";
$myCar->year = 2022;

echo $myCar->make . " " . $myCar->model . " " . $myCar->year; //
Outputs: "Toyota Camry 2022"
echo $myCar->startEngine(); // Outputs: "The engine has started."
```

It is also possible to define properties and methods with visibility keywords such as `public`, `private`, and `protected`. This allows us to control the accessibility of class members and enforce encapsulation. For example:

```php
class Car {
  private $make;
  public $model;
  protected $year;

  function startEngine() {
    return "The engine has started.";
  }
}


$myCar = new Car();
$myCar->make = "Toyota"; // This will result in an error, because
the make property has private visibility
$myCar->model = "Camry";
$myCar->year = 2022; // This will result in an error, because the
year property has protected visibility

echo $myCar->model; // Outputs: "Camry"
echo $myCar->startEngine(); // Outputs: "The engine has started."
```

6.3 Constructors and Destructors

Constructors and destructors are special methods in a class that are automatically executed when an object of the class is created or destroyed, respectively. Constructors are used to initialize class properties and perform any necessary setup when an object is created. Destructors are used to perform any necessary cleanup when an object is destroyed.

In PHP, the name of a constructor method must be the same as the name of the class. For example, if you have a class named "Person", the constructor method would be named "Person".

Here's an example of how you can use a constructor in PHP:

```php
class Person {
  public $name;
  public $age;

  function __construct($name, $age) {
    $this->name = $name;
```

```
      $this->age = $age;
  }

  function sayHello() {
    echo "Hello, my name is " . $this->name . " and I am " .
$this->age . " years old.";
  }
}

$person = new Person("John", 30);
$person->sayHello(); // Output: "Hello, my name is John and I am
30 years old."
```

In this example, the constructor method `__construct` initializes the `$name` and `$age` properties of the `Person` class. When an object of the `Person` class is created, the constructor is automatically called and the properties are set accordingly.

Destructors work similarly to constructors, but they are called when an object is destroyed. In PHP, the name of a destructor method is `__destruct`. Here's an example of how you can use a destructor in PHP:

```
class Person {
  public $name;

  function __construct($name) {
    $this->name = $name;
  }

  function __destruct() {
    echo "Goodbye, " . $this->name . "!";
  }
}

$person = new Person("John");
unset($person); // Output: "Goodbye, John!"
```

In this example, the destructor method `__destruct` is automatically called when the `$person` object is destroyed by using the `unset` function. The destructor outputs a goodbye message for the person.

Constructors and destructors are useful for performing actions when an object is created or destroyed, and they are an important part of object-oriented programming in PHP.

6.4: Inheritance and Polymorphism

Inheritance is a fundamental concept in object-oriented programming. It refers to the ability of a class to inherit properties and methods from a parent class. This allows you to create a new class that builds upon an existing class, without having to rewrite all of its code. The new class is called a derived class or a subclass, and the class it inherits from is called the base class or the superclass.

For example, let's consider a class "Vehicle" that has properties such as the number of wheels, the number of doors, and the type of engine. You could then create a derived class called "Car" that inherits from the "Vehicle" class and adds its own properties, such as the number of seats.

```
class Vehicle {
    public $wheels;
    public $doors;
    public $engine;

    public function __construct($wheels, $doors, $engine) {
        $this->wheels = $wheels;
        $this->doors = $doors;
        $this->engine = $engine;
    }
}

class Car extends Vehicle {
    public $seats;

    public function __construct($wheels, $doors, $engine, $seats)
    {
        parent::__construct($wheels, $doors, $engine);
        $this->seats = $seats;
    }
}
$myCar = new Car(4, 4, "gasoline", 5);
echo $myCar->wheels; // outputs 4
echo $myCar->seats; // outputs 5
```

Polymorphism refers to the ability of a class to have multiple forms. This is achieved through method overriding, where a subclass can provide a new implementation for a method that it has inherited from the parent class.

For example, consider the class "Animal" with a method called `makeSound()`. You could then create a derived class called "Dog" that overrides the `makeSound()` method to provide a new implementation that outputs the sound a dog makes.

```php
class Animal {
    public function makeSound() {
        echo "This is the sound made by an animal";
    }
}

class Dog extends Animal {
    public function makeSound() {
        echo "Woof!";
    }
}

$myDog = new Dog();
$myDog->makeSound(); // outputs "Woof!"
```

Inheritance and polymorphism are powerful features in object-oriented programming that allow you to create complex and dynamic applications. Understanding these concepts and how to use them effectively is essential for any PHP developer.

6.5: The Scope Resolution operator

The scope resolution operator `::` is a unique operator in PHP that allows access to static, constant, and overridden properties and methods of a class. It allows you to define class properties and methods that are shared across all instances of a class, as well as to access inherited properties and methods from a parent class.

○ **Static Properties and Methods**

In PHP, a static property or method is defined using the keyword "static". When a property or method is defined as static, it is shared across all instances of a class and can be accessed without creating an instance of the class. The scope resolution operator `::` is used to access static properties and methods, for example:

```php
class Car {
    public static $numberOfCars = 0;
    public static function getNumberOfCars() {
        return self::$numberOfCars;
    }
}
```

```
// Accessing static properties and methods
echo Car::$numberOfCars;
echo Car::getNumberOfCars();
```

○ Constant Properties

In PHP, a constant property is a property that cannot be changed once it has been set. Constants are defined using the keyword "const", and the scope resolution operator `::` is used to access constant properties, for example:

```
class Circle {
  const PI = 3.14;
}
// Accessing constant properties echo Circle::PI;
```

○ Parent Class Properties and Methods

The scope resolution operator `::` can also be used to access properties and methods from a parent class. This is particularly useful when you want to override a method in a subclass, but still have access to the original implementation in the parent class. For example:

```
class Vehicle {
  public function startEngine() {
    echo "Vehicle engine started.";
  }
}
class Car extends Vehicle {
  public function startEngine() {
    echo "Car engine started.";
  }
  public function accessParentEngine() {
    parent::startEngine();
  }
}
$car = new Car();
$car->startEngine(); // Outputs: "Car engine started."
$car->accessParentEngine(); // Outputs: "Vehicle engine started."
```

Understanding the scope resolution operator is important when working with classes and objects in PHP, as it provides a convenient and flexible way to access and manipulate class properties and methods.

Chapter 7: Working with Forms and Handling Inputs

7.1 Creating and Processing HTML Forms

In this subchapter, you will learn about creating HTML forms and processing user input using PHP. A form is an essential component of any web application that requires user input, such as search forms, feedback forms, login forms, and more.

○ Creating a Basic HTML Form

HTML forms are created using the `<form>` element and its various attributes, such as action and method. The `action` attribute specifies the URL of the PHP script that will process the form data, while the method attribute specifies the HTTP method used to submit the form data (GET or POST). Here is a basic example of an HTML form:

```
<form action="process_form.php" method="post">
  <label for="username">Username:</label>
  <input type="text" id="username" name="username">
  <br><br>
  <label for="password">Password:</label>
  <input type="password" id="password" name="password">
  <br><br>
  <input type="submit" value="Submit">
</form>
```

○ Processing HTML Form Data with PHP

Once the form data is submitted, it can be processed using a PHP script. The PHP script can access the form data using the `$_POST` or `$_GET` superglobal arrays, depending on the HTTP method used to submit the form.

Here is an example of how you can process the form data from the previous example:

```
if ($_SERVER['REQUEST_METHOD'] == 'POST') {
  $username = $_POST['username'];
  $password = $_POST['password'];

  // process the form data here
  echo "Username: " . $username . "<br>";
  echo "Password: " . $password;
}
```

7.2 Understanding GET and POST Method

When sending data from a form to a web server, the two most common methods used are the `GET` and `POST` methods. It is important to understand the difference between the two and when to use each.

○ **GET Method**

The `GET` method appends form data to the URL in the form of query strings. It is typically used to retrieve data from the server or to send simple data to the server. The data sent using the `GET` method is visible in the URL and is limited in size. As a result, the `GET` method is not suitable for sending sensitive information such as passwords or credit card numbers.

For example, consider a simple search form that allows the user to search for a keyword on a website. The form might look something like this:

```
<form action="search.php" method="get">
  <input type="text" name="keyword">
  <input type="submit" value="Search">
</form>
```

When the user submits the form, the data is appended to the URL in the following format:

```
http://www.example.com/search.php?keyword=search_term
```

○ **POST Method**

The `POST` method sends form data in the body of the HTTP request. This method is more secure and flexible than the `GET` method because it does not have any size limitations and the data is not visible in the URL. The `POST` method is typically used when sending sensitive data such as passwords or credit card numbers to the server.

For example consider a simple registration form that allows the user to create an account on a website. The form might look something like this:

```
<form action="register.php" method="post">
  <input type="text" name="username">
  <input type="password" name="password">
  <input type="submit" value="Register">
</form>
```

When the user submits the form, the data is sent to the server in the body of the HTTP request and is not visible in the URL.

In conclusion, the `GET` method is best used for simple and non-sensitive data transfers, while the `POST` method is suitable for sending more complex and sensitive data to the server.

7.3 Validating and Sanitizing User Input

When receiving data from a form, it is important to validate and sanitize the user input to ensure the data received is both safe and accurate. This is critical in preventing security vulnerabilities such as SQL injection or cross-site scripting (XSS) attacks.

○ **Validation**

Validation is the process of checking if the data received meets the specified criteria. For example, checking if a text field is not empty, or if a date is in the correct format. In PHP, this can be done using functions such as `isset()`, `empty()`, and `preg_match()`.

For example, consider a simple form that allows the user to enter their age. The form might look something like this:

```
<form action="submit.php" method="post">
  <input type="text" name="age">
  <input type="submit" value="Submit">
</form>
```

In the processing script, the age can be validated as follows:

```
if (isset($_POST["age"]) && !empty($_POST["age"])) {
  if (preg_match("/^[0-9]+$/", $_POST["age"])) {
    echo "Valid Age";
  } else {
    echo "Invalid Age";
  }
} else {
  echo "Age is required";
}
```

○ **Sanitization**

Sanitization is the process of cleaning or transforming the data to make it safe to use. For example, removing any HTML tags from a text field. In PHP, this can be done using functions such as `htmlspecialchars()` and `strip_tags()`.

For example, consider a simple form that allows the user to enter a message. The form might look something like this:

```
<form action="submit.php" method="post">
  <textarea name="message"></textarea>
  <input type="submit" value="Submit">
</form>
```

In the processing script, the message can be sanitized as follows:

```
if (isset($_POST["message"]) && !empty($_POST["message"])) {
  $message = htmlspecialchars($_POST["message"]);
  echo $message;
} else {
  echo "Message is required";
}
```

In conclusion, it's important to validate and sanitize user input to ensure that the data received is both accurate and safe to use. This helps to prevent security vulnerabilities and improve the overall quality of the application.

7.4 Handling file uploads

One of the common requirements for web applications is the ability to allow users to upload files. This can include images, documents, videos, etc. PHP provides the `$_FILES` superglobal array to handle file uploads.

Before you start handling file uploads, you should set the maximum size of uploaded files in your PHP configuration file using the `upload_max_filesize` directive. You should also consider setting the maximum allowed time for uploading a file using the `max_input_time directive`.

To handle file uploads, you need to create an HTML form with a file input element, and then handle the uploaded file on the server-side.

For example, consider a simple form that allows the user to upload an image. The form might look something like this:

```
<form action="submit.php" method="post" enctype="multipart/
form-data">
  <input type="file" name="image">
  <input type="submit" value="Submit">
</form>
```

Note the use of the enctype attribute set to multipart/form-data. This is necessary when uploading files using the `POST` method.

In the processing script, the uploaded file can be handled as follows:

```php
if (isset($_FILES["image"]) && $_FILES["image"]["error"] == 0) {
  $file = $_FILES["image"];
  $allowed = array("jpg" => "image/jpg", "jpeg" => "image/jpeg",
"gif" => "image/gif", "png" => "image/png");
  $filename = $file["name"];
  $filetype = $file["type"];
  $filesize = $file["size"];
  $ext = pathinfo($filename, PATHINFO_EXTENSION);
  if (!array_key_exists($ext, $allowed)) {
    echo "Error: Please select a valid file format.";
  } else {
    $maxsize = 5 * 1024 * 1024;
    if ($filesize > $maxsize) {
      echo "Error: File size is larger than the allowed limit.";
    } else {
      $target_dir = "uploads/";
      $target_file = $target_dir . basename($filename);
      if (move_uploaded_file($file["tmp_name"], $target_file)) {
        echo "The file ". basename( $filename). " has been upload-
ed.";
      } else {
        echo "Error: There was an error uploading your file.
Please try again.";
      }
    }
  }
} else {
  echo "Error: Please select a file to upload.";
}
```

In the example above, we check if the file input is not empty and if there are no errors with the uploaded file. Then, we check if the file type is allowed and if the file size is within the allowed limit. Finally, we move the uploaded file to a specified directory using the `move_uploaded_file()` function.

In conclusion, handling file uploads in PHP is straightforward and can be achieved with just a few lines of code. It is important to validate the uploaded file type and size to ensure that only acceptable files are processed and stored on the server. This helps maintain the security and integrity of your web application and prevents any potential security risks, such as uploading malicious files.

Chapter 8: Working with Forms and Handling Inputs

8.1 Understanding Relational Databases and SQL

A relational database is a collection of data organized into tables with rows and columns. The relationships between tables are established using keys, and this structure is called a relational model. SQL (Structured Query Language) is a standard language used to communicate with and manipulate relational databases.

In a relational database, each table represents a different type of data, and each row represents a single instance of that data. For example, a table named "customers" might have columns for "customer_id", "name", "email", and "address", and each row would represent a different customer.

Relational databases allow you to store and retrieve data in a structured and organized manner, and provide the ability to query and manipulate data in complex ways. This makes relational databases a popular choice for many web applications.

SQL is used to perform various operations on relational databases, such as creating tables, inserting data, updating data, retrieving data, and deleting data.

Example:

Consider a simple relational database for a book store. The database might have two tables: "books" and "authors". The "books" table would have columns for "book_id", "title", "author_id", "price", and "quantity", and each row would represent a different book. The "authors" table would have columns for "author_id", "first_name", "last_name", and "nationality", and each row would represent a different author.

To retrieve data from this database, you could use a SQL query like this:

```
SELECT books.title, authors.first_name, authors.last_name
FROM books
JOIN authors
ON books.author_id = authors.author_id
```

This query would return a table with columns for "title", "first_name", and "last_name", and each row would represent a book and its author.

Relational databases and SQL are essential tools for storing and managing data in a structured and efficient manner. Understanding the relational model and the basics of SQL is a key skill for developing robust and scalable web applications.

8.2 Connecting to a Database using PHP

To interact with a relational database in a PHP web application, you need to establish a connection between the PHP script and the database. The PHP extension `mysqli` (MySQL Improved) provides an easy-to-use interface for connecting to and manipulating MySQL databases.

To connect to a database using PHP, you will need the following information:

• **Hostname**: the domain name or IP address of the database server

• **Database name**: the name of the database you want to connect to

• **username**: the username for connecting to the database

• **password**: the password for connecting to the database

Here's an example of how to connect to a MySQL database using the `mysqli` extension in PHP:

```php
<?php
$hostname = "localhost";
$database = "bookstore";
$username = "root";
$password = "secret";

// Create a connection to the database
$conn = mysqli_connect($hostname, $username, $password, $data-
base);

// Check if the connection was successful
if (!$conn) {
    die("Connection failed: " . mysqli_connect_error());
}

// The connection was successful, we can now use the $conn object
to interact with the database

// Close the connection when we're done
mysqli_close($conn);
?>
```

In this example, we are connecting to a MySQL database named "bookstore" on the local machine using the username "root" and password "secret". The `mysqli_connect` function returns a connection object that we can use to interact with the database, and the `mysqli_close` function is used to close the connection when we're done.

It's important to note that for security reasons, you should never store sensitive information, such as database passwords, in your source code. Instead, you should store such information in a separate configuration file and include it in your scripts as needed.

Connecting to a database using PHP and the `mysqli` extension is a straightforward process, and with a little bit of code, you can start working with your data and storing it in a relational database.

8.3 Executing SQL queries and commands

Once you have established a connection to a database, you can start executing SQL queries and commands to interact with your data. SQL (Structured Query Language) is the language used to manipulate data in relational databases.

The most common types of SQL commands are `SELECT`, `INSERT`, `UPDATE`, and `DELETE`. These commands allow you to retrieve data from a database, add new data, modify existing data, and remove data, respectively.

Here's an example of how to execute a `SELECT` query using the `mysqli` extension in PHP:

```php
<?php
$hostname = "localhost";
$database = "bookstore";
$username = "root";
$password = "secret";

// Create a connection to the database
$conn = mysqli_connect($hostname, $username, $password, $data-
base);

// Check if the connection was successful
if (!$conn) {
    die("Connection failed: " . mysqli_connect_error());
}

// The connection was successful, we can now use the $conn object
to interact with the database

// Define the SQL query
$sql = "SELECT title, author, publication_year FROM books";

// Execute the query
$result = mysqli_query($conn, $sql);
```

```php
// Check if the query was successful
if (!$result) {
    die("Query failed: " . mysqli_error($conn));
}

// The query was successful, we can now fetch the results
while ($row = mysqli_fetch_assoc($result)) {
    echo "Title: " . $row['title'] . " Author: " . $row['author']
. " Year: " . $row['publication_year'] . "<br>";
}

// Close the connection when we're done
mysqli_close($conn);
?>
```

In this example, we are connecting to a MySQL database named "bookstore" and executing a `SELECT` query that retrieves the title, author, and publication year of books from the books table. The `mysqli_query` function is used to execute the query, and the `mysqli_fetch_assoc` function is used to fetch the results one row at a time.

Similarly, you can execute other SQL commands, such as `INSERT`, `UPDATE`, and `DELETE`, using the `mysqli_query` function. Here's an example of how to execute an `INSERT` command:

```php
<?php
$hostname = "localhost";
$database = "bookstore";
$username = "root";
$password = "secret";

// Create a connection to the database
$conn = mysqli_connect($hostname, $username, $password, $database);

// Check if the connection was successful
if (!$conn) {
    die("Connection failed: " . mysqli_connect_error());
}

// The connection was successful, we can now use the $conn object
to interact with the database

// Define the SQL command
```

```php
$sql = "INSERT INTO books (title, author, publication_year) VALUES
('The Great Gatsby', 'F. Scott Fitzgerald', 1925)";

// Execute the command
$result = mysqli_query($conn, $sql);

// Check if the command was successful
if ($result) {
    echo "Record inserted successfully.";
} else {
    echo "Error inserting record: " . mysqli_error($conn);
}

// Close the connection when we're done
mysqli_close($conn);
?>
```

In this example, we are connecting to the same database as before and executing an `INSERT` command that adds a new book to the books table. The `mysqli_query` function is used to execute the command, and the `mysqli_error` function is used to retrieve error information in case the command fails. If the command is successful, a message "Record inserted successfully." will be displayed.

It's important to keep in mind that when executing SQL commands, it's possible to introduce security vulnerabilities if the commands are not properly sanitized. To prevent this, you can use prepared statements and parameter binding to avoid SQL injection attacks.

8.4 Working with query results

Here's an example of how you can work with query results in PHP using the `mysqli` extension:

```php
<?php
// Connect to the database
$conn = mysqli_connect("localhost", "username", "password", "database_name");

// Check if the connection was successful
if (!$conn) {
    die("Connection failed: " . mysqli_connect_error());
}
```

```php
// Execute a SELECT query
$sql = "SELECT id, title, author FROM books";
$result = mysqli_query($conn, $sql);

// Check if the query was successful
if (mysqli_num_rows($result) > 0) {
    // Output the results
    while ($row = mysqli_fetch_assoc($result)) {
        echo "ID: " . $row["id"] . " - Title: " . $row["title"] .
" - Author: " . $row["author"] . "<br>";
    }
} else {
    echo "No results found.";
}

// Close the connection when we're done
mysqli_close($conn);
?>
```

In this example, we connect to a database and execute a `SELECT` query to retrieve information about books from the books table. The `mysqli_query` function is used to execute the query, and the `mysqli_num_rows` function is used to check if the query returned any results. If the query was successful and returned one or more rows, the results are outputted using a `while` loop and the `mysqli_fetch_assoc` function, which retrieves the next row as an associative array. The `mysqli_fetch_assoc` function should be called in a `loop` until it returns `NULL`, which indicates that all rows have been retrieved.

Keep in mind that when working with query results, it's important to properly handle errors and check for results to avoid potential bugs in your code.

Chapter 9: Working with Forms and Handling Inputs

9.1 Understanding common error types

In PHP, there are several common error types that you'll likely encounter when developing your applications. Understanding these error types can help you diagnose and fix problems more effectively.

○ **Syntax errors**

This type of error occurs when there is a problem with the syntax of your code, such as a missing semicolon or a typo. Syntax errors will cause your code to fail immediately and will prevent the script from executing. For example:

```php
<?php
echo "Hello, World!"
?>
```

In this example, there's a missing semicolon after the `echo` statement, which will result in a syntax error.

○ **Notice errors**

This type of error occurs when there is a problem with the logic of your code, such as accessing an undefined variable. Notice errors are less severe than other types of errors, but they can still cause problems if not addressed. For example:

```php
<?php
$name = "John Doe";
echo "Hello, $nam";
?>
```

In this example, the variable $nam is misspelled and does not match the defined variable $name, which will result in a notice error.

○ **Warning errors**

This type of error occurs when there is a problem with a function or operation, such as trying to open a file that doesn't exist. Warning errors will cause your code to continue executing, but they can cause unexpected results if not addressed.

```php
<?php
$file = fopen("nonexistent.txt", "r");
?>
```

In this example, the fopen function is trying to open a file that doesn't exist, which will result in a warning error.

○ **Fatal errors**

This type of error occurs when there is a problem that prevents your code from continuing to execute, such as trying to call a function that doesn't exist. Fatal errors will stop your code from executing and display an error message.

```php
<?php
nonexistent_function();
?>
```

In this example, the `nonexistent_function` does not exist, which will result in a fatal error.

By understanding these common error types, you'll be better equipped to diagnose and fix problems in your code.

9.2 Debugging techniques and tools

In PHP, there are several techniques and tools that can help you debug your code and identify problems.

○ **'error_reporting'**

This function allows you to control the level of error reporting in your code. By default, all error types are reported, but you can use this function to suppress certain types of errors or to display only specific types of errors.

```php
<?php
error_reporting(E_ERROR | E_WARNING | E_PARSE);
echo "Hello, World!";
nonexistent_function();
?>
```

In this example, the `error_reporting` function is used to display only `E_ERROR`, `E_WARNING`, and `E_PARSE` errors. As a result, the `nonexistent_function` error will not be displayed.

○ **'var_dump'**

This function allows you to inspect the contents of a variable, including its type and value. You can use `var_dump` to identify problems with your code, such as incorrect variable types or unexpected values.

```php
<?php
$name = "John Doe";
var_dump($name);
?>
```

In this example, the `var_dump` function is used to inspect the contents of the $name variable. The output will show the type (string) and value ("John Doe") of the variable.

○ **'debug_backtrace'**

This function allows you to trace the execution of your code and identify where errors are occurring. You can use `debug_backtrace` to see the function call stack and determine the sequence of function calls that led to the error.

```php
<?php
function do_something() {
    debug_backtrace();
}

function call_do_something() {
    do_something();
}

call_do_something();
?>
```

In this example, the `debug_backtrace` function is used to trace the execution of the code. The output will show the sequence of function calls that led to the `debug_backtrace` function, including the functions `call_do_something` and `do_something`.

These are just a few of the many debugging techniques and tools available in PHP. By using these tools and techniques, you can quickly and effectively identify and fix problems in your code.

9.3 Exception handling and try/catch

Exception handling is an important aspect of error handling in PHP. It allows you to catch and handle errors in a structured and organized way, rather than relying on error reporting or other debugging techniques.

The basic syntax for exception handling in PHP is to use the try and catch blocks. You place your code that may generate an error in the try block, and specify how to handle the error in the catch block.

```php
<?php
try {
    $file = fopen("nonexistent_file.txt", "r");
} catch (Exception $e) {
```

```
        echo "An error occurred: " . $e->getMessage();
}
?>
```

In this example, an error will occur when trying to open the nonexistent file `nonexistent_file.txt`. The error is caught by the catch block, which displays a message indicating that an error occurred and includes the error message.

You can also throw your own exceptions in your code, which can be caught and handled by a catch block. This allows you to implement custom error handling logic, such as providing more specific error messages or performing specific actions based on the type of error that occurred.

```
<?php
function divide($a, $b) {
    if ($b == 0) {
        throw new Exception("Cannot divide by zero");
    }
    return $a / $b;
}

try {
    $result = divide(10, 0);
    echo $result;
} catch (Exception $e) {
    echo "An error occurred: " . $e->getMessage();
}
?>
```

In this example, the `divide` function throws an exception when dividing by zero. The exception is caught and handled by the `catch` block, which displays a custom error message indicating that the division by zero error occurred.

By using `exception` handling in your code, you can write more robust and error-resistant applications that are better equipped to handle unexpected errors and exceptions.

9.4 Exception Handling and try/catch

Logging and tracing are important techniques for debugging and troubleshooting in PHP. Logging involves recording information about the events and actions that occur in your application, while tracing involves recording information about the execution flow and performance of your application.

In PHP, you can implement logging and tracing by using the built-in functions `error_log` and `debug_backtrace`, respectively.

```php
<?php
// Logging with error_log
error_log("An error occurred while processing a request");

// Tracing with debug_backtrace
function foo() {
    bar();
}

function bar() {
    $trace = debug_backtrace();
    print_r($trace);
}

foo();
```

In this example, the `error_log` function is used to log an error message. The `debug_backtrace` function is used to print a trace of the function calls that occurred in the script.

You can also configure PHP to write logs to specific locations, such as a file or a syslog server, by setting the `error_log` configuration directive in your `php.ini` file.

```
; php.ini
error_log = "/var/log/php_errors.log"
```

In this example, PHP is configured to write log messages to the file `/var/log/php_errors.log`.

By using `logging` and `tracing` in your PHP applications, you can gain valuable insights into the behavior and performance of your code, and quickly identify and resolve issues that arise.

Chapter 10: Advanced Topics: Security and Performance Optimization

10.1 Understanding common security risks and vulnerabilities

In web development, security is a critical aspect to consider, as applications can be vulnerable to various security risks and vulnerabilities that can lead to data breaches, loss of sensitive information, and other serious consequences.

Some of the common security risks and vulnerabilities in PHP include SQL Injection, Cross-Site Scripting (XSS), Cross-Site Request Forgery (CSRF)

○ **SQL Injection**

An attack where malicious code is inserted into an SQL statement to manipulate the data stored in a database.

```php
<?php
// Vulnerable code
$id = $_GET['id'];
$sql = "SELECT * FROM users WHERE id = $id";
$result = mysqli_query($conn, $sql);
```

In this example, a user could manipulate the `id` parameter in the URL to inject malicious code into the SQL statement, potentially compromising the data stored in the database.

○ **Cross-Site Scripting (XSS)**

An attack where malicious scripts are injected into a web page viewed by other users.

```php
<?php
// Vulnerable code
$name = $_GET['name'];
echo "Hello, $name!";
```

In this example, a user could manipulate the `name` parameter in the URL to inject a malicious script into the web page, potentially compromising the security of other users who view the page.

○ **Cross-Site Request Forgery (CSRF)**

An attack where a malicious website tricks a user into performing an unintended action on another website.

```php
<?php
// Vulnerable code
if ($_POST['submit']) {
    update_user_password($_POST['password']);
}
```

In this example, a malicious website could trick a user into submitting a form that updates their password on another website, compromising the security of their account.

To prevent these and other security risks and vulnerabilities, it is important to follow best practices for secure coding, such as using parameterized queries, sanitizing user input, and implementing proper authentication and authorization mechanisms.

10.2 Implementing Best Practices for Secure Coding

In this subchapter, we will discuss some of the best practices for secure coding in PHP that can help prevent security vulnerabilities and protect sensitive data.

Here are some of the key areas to focus on:

1. **Input validation**: Validate all user input, including form data, query string parameters, and other data coming from the client. Use the appropriate functions, such as `filter_var()` and `preg_match()`, to validate the type and format of the input.

2. **Escape output**: When displaying user-generated content, escape any special characters to prevent Cross-Site Scripting (XSS) attacks. Use `htmlentities()` or `htmlspecialchars()` to escape any HTML characters.

3. **Use encryption**: Whenever possible, encrypt sensitive data before storing it in the database. Use the `mcrypt` library or other encryption libraries to encrypt data.

4. **Use prepared statements**: To prevent SQL Injection attacks, use prepared statements instead of concatenating strings to form SQL commands. The prepared statements provide a secure way to insert user input into the database.

5. **Avoid storing sensitive data**: Avoid storing sensitive data, such as passwords, in plain text. Instead, store hashes of the passwords and use salted hashes for added security.

6. **Keep software up-to-date**: Regularly check for and apply security patches for all software and libraries used in the application.

7. **Sanitize files**: When uploading files to the server, validate the file type and size before accepting the upload. Use `unlink()` to delete uploaded files that are not needed.

8. **Use secure connections**: When transmitting sensitive data, use secure connections, such as `HTTPS`, to prevent eavesdropping and tampering of the data.

By following these best practices, you can help ensure the security of your PHP applications and protect sensitive data. Of course, this is by no means an exhaustive list, and there may be other steps specific to your application that you will need to take.

10.3 Techniques for Performance Optimization

Performance optimization is an essential aspect of web development, as it can significantly impact the user experience and overall performance of a web application.

Here are some techniques for performance optimization in PHP:

1. **Minimize the number of database queries**: Accessing a database is a time-consuming operation, so it's best to minimize the number of database queries as much as possible. You can cache the results of frequently-used queries in memory, or use a caching mechanism such as `APC` (Alternative PHP Cache) or `Memcached` to store results for a specified amount of time.

2. **Use prepared statements**: Prepared statements are a feature of the database that allow you to send a template of a query, along with placeholders for dynamic data, to the database server. This eliminates the need to escape and concatenate dynamic data into the query string, reducing the risk of SQL injection attacks and improving performance.

3. **Optimize your code**: Use techniques such as code `profiling`, `benchmarking`, and `load testing` to identify the bottlenecks in your code. Optimize the most critical parts of your code, such as the database queries, loops, and function calls, to improve performance.

4. **Compress and minify assets**: Compressing and minifying your assets, such as HTML, CSS, and JavaScript files, can significantly reduce their file size, thus reducing the time required to transfer them to the user's browser.

5. **Use a Content Delivery Network (CDN)**: A CDN is a network of servers that store and deliver content, such as images and videos, to users based on their location. By using a CDN, you can distribute the load of serving assets,

reducing the load on your server and improving the performance of your web application.

Here is an example:

```php
<?php
// Use prepared statements to execute database queries
$stmt = $conn->prepare("SELECT * FROM users WHERE name = ?");
$stmt->bind_param("s", $name);
$stmt->execute();

// Compress and minify HTML content
ob_start("ob_gzhandler");
?>
<!DOCTYPE html>
<html>
<head>
  <meta charset="UTF-8">
  <title>Performance Optimization Example</title>
</head>
<body>
  <h1>Performance Optimization Example</h1>
  <p>Welcome to the world of performance optimization!</p>
</body>
</html>
<?php
ob_end_flush();
?>
```

10.4 Understanding caching and memory management

Caching and memory management are important topics for optimizing the performance of PHP applications. Caching can significantly improve the speed and responsiveness of a website by storing frequently used data in memory, reducing the number of database queries and computations required. Memory management, on the other hand, helps ensure that your PHP application uses available memory efficiently and avoids memory leaks that can cause performance issues.

○ **Caching**

Caching is the process of storing frequently used data in memory to avoid recalculating or re-fetching it each time it is needed. This helps reduce the number of database queries and computation-intensive operations, leading to improved performance.

There are several types of caching that can be used in PHP applications, including:

• **Opcode caching**: This caches the compiled version of PHP scripts to avoid recompilation each time the script is executed. Opcode caches like APC, OpCache, and Zend Optimizer+ can significantly improve the performance of PHP applications.

• **Page caching**: This caches the entire output of a dynamic web page, allowing the cached version to be served directly to the user instead of re-generating the page each time it is requested.

• **Object caching**: This caches objects, arrays, or other data structures in memory for faster access.

○ **Memory Management**

Memory management refers to the process of controlling the use of memory within a PHP application. Good memory management helps ensure that the application uses available memory efficiently and avoids memory leaks, which can cause performance issues over time.

To improve memory management in PHP, you can use techniques such as:

• **Unsetting variables**: Unsetting variables when they are no longer needed can help release memory that would otherwise be retained by the application.

• **Using garbage collection**: PHP has a built-in garbage collector that automatically frees memory that is no longer needed by the application. Enabling garbage collection can help improve memory management in PHP.

• **Monitoring memory usage**: Using tools such as `memory_get_peak_usage()` can help you monitor the memory usage of your PHP application and identify areas where memory optimization is needed.

```php
<?php
// Unsetting a variable
$name = 'John Doe';
echo memory_get_usage(), "\n";
unset($name);
echo memory_get_usage(), "\n";

// Using garbage collection
gc_enable();
$array = range(1, 100000);
```

```php
unset($array);
gc_collect_cycles();
echo memory_get_usage(), "\n";

// Monitoring memory usage
function process_data() {
  $data = range(1, 100000);
  echo memory_get_peak_usage(), "\n";
  unset($data);
}

process_data();
echo memory_get_usage(), "\n";
```

In this example, we first unset the `$name` variable to release the memory it was using. Next, we enable garbage collection and run `gc_collect_cycles()` to free any memory that is no longer needed. Finally, we use `memory_get_peak_usage()` to monitor the memory usage of the `process_data()` function and ensure that memory is being released when it is no longer needed.

Chapter 11: Building and Deploying a PHP Web Application

11.1 Understanding the development process and deployment pipeline

The development process of a PHP web application is a series of stages that includes planning, designing, coding, testing, and deploying. Understanding this process and the steps involved is crucial for building and deploying a successful application.

A deployment pipeline is a set of automated processes that enable developers to build, test, and deploy their applications. This pipeline ensures that changes made to the code are thoroughly tested and validated before being released to production.

The following are the stages in the development process and deployment pipeline:

• **Planning**: In this stage, the project requirements and goals are defined, and the project team is assembled.

• **Designing**: This stage involves creating a high-level design of the application, including the architecture and user interface.

• **Coding**: In this stage, the developers write the code that implements the design. They should also write automated tests to validate the functionality of the application.

• **Testing**: In this stage, the code is tested to ensure that it meets the requirements and goals defined in the planning stage. Automated tests and manual tests can be used to validate the functionality of the application.

• **Deployment**: After the code has been thoroughly tested, it can be deployed to a web server for production use. This stage involves configuring the server, setting up the database, and deploying the application.

By understanding the development process and deployment pipeline, developers can build, test, and deploy their applications more effectively. This leads to faster delivery of high-quality applications that meet the needs of their users.

11.2 Setting up a Development and Production Environment

Setting up a proper environment is crucial for the development and deployment of a PHP web application. It involves creating a local development environment and a separate production environment that are isolated from each other. The local development environment is used to build and test the application, while the production environment is used to host the application for end-users.

Creating a Development Environment

A local development environment can be created on a computer using a web server software such as Apache or Nginx, and a database management system such as MySQL. A popular and free solution for setting up a local development environment is to use the XAMPP software, which includes Apache, MySQL, and PHP, as well as other tools.

Another option is to use virtualization software, such as VirtualBox or Vagrant, to create a virtual machine that can be used as the development environment. This method offers more flexibility and is suitable for teams working on the same project.

Setting up a Production Environment

When the application is ready for deployment, it is essential to set up a separate production environment that is optimized for performance and security. This typically involves renting a web server from a hosting provider and configuring it to host the application.

It's important to ensure that the production environment is secure and regularly updated with the latest security patches and software versions. This helps to prevent common security threats, such as SQL injection attacks, cross-site scripting (XSS), and cross-site request forgery (CSRF).

For example, you can set up a development environment using XAMPP on a Windows computer. After downloading and installing XAMPP, you can start the Apache and MySQL services, and place your PHP files in the htdocs directory of the XAMPP installation. You can then access your PHP application using a web browser by visiting `http://localhost`.

For the production environment, you can rent a web server from a hosting provider, such as Bluehost or HostGator, and configure it to host your PHP application. This typically involves uploading your PHP files to the server, creating a database, and configuring the PHP settings to match your development environment. After deploying the application, you can access it from anywhere by visiting the domain name associated with the web server.

11.3 Building and Testing a PHP Web Application

This subchapter will focus on the process of building and testing a PHP web application from start to finish. This process is essential to ensure that the application meets all the required specifications and functions as intended.

The first step in building a PHP web application is to determine the requirements of the application. This involves defining the objectives, goals, and scope of the project. This will help to determine the specific features and functionalities that need to be included in the application.

Once the requirements have been defined, the next step is to design the architecture of the application. This involves creating a blueprint of the application, including the data model, the database schema, and the user interface.

Next, the actual development of the application can begin. This involves writing the code that implements the features and functionalities defined in the requirements. It is important to write clean, well-documented code that follows best practices for PHP development.

After the code has been written, it is time to test the application. This involves running the application and verifying that it functions as expected. This can be done manually by navigating through the application and testing each feature, or it can be automated using testing frameworks such as PHPUnit.

It is important to thoroughly test the application to identify and fix any bugs or issues that may arise. This will help to ensure that the application is reliable and performs well in a production environment.

In conclusion, building and testing a PHP web application is a crucial step in the development process. It requires careful planning, attention to detail, and thorough testing to ensure that the application meets all the requirements and functions as intended.

11.4 Deploying to a Web Server

Deploying a PHP web application to a web server involves copying the application's code, database, and configuration files from the development environment to the production environment. Here are the steps involved in deploying a PHP web application to a web server:

• **Backup your database**: Before deploying your application, make sure to backup your database. This will ensure that you have a copy of the database data in case something goes wrong during the deployment process.

• **Copy the code**: Using a FTP client such as FileZilla, copy the PHP code and other assets (e.g. images, CSS, JavaScript) from the development environment to the production environment.

• **Configure the database**: Update the database configuration file with the correct credentials for the production environment. This file should contain the database hostname, username, password, and database name.

• **Verify the configuration**: Open the application in a web browser and check if the configuration is working correctly. Make sure that the database connection is successful and that the application is able to retrieve data from the database.

• **Test the application**: Thoroughly test the application in the production environment to ensure that everything is working correctly. Check for any bugs, errors or issues that may have been introduced during the deployment process.

• **Monitor the application**: After deploying the application, it's important to monitor it to make sure that it's functioning correctly. You can use tools such as error logs, performance monitoring software, and system monitoring software to keep an eye on the application and ensure that it's running smoothly.

For example let's say you have a simple PHP application that allows users to submit blog posts and view a list of all blog posts. To deploy this application to a web server, you would follow these steps:

• **Backup your database**: Use the mysqldump command to backup the database.

• **Copy the code**: Use an FTP client such as FileZilla to copy the PHP code, HTML, CSS and JavaScript files from the development environment to the production environment.

• **Configure the database**: Open the database configuration file and update the database credentials with the correct values for the production environment.

• **Verify the configuration**: Open the application in a web browser and check if the database connection is successful and if the application is able to retrieve data from the database.

• **Test the application**: Test the application thoroughly to make sure that everything is working correctly. Check that users are able to submit blog posts, view a list of all blog posts, and that the application is free of bugs and errors.

• **Monitor the application**: Use tools such as error logs, performance monitoring software, and system monitoring software to monitor the application and ensure that it's functioning correctly.

Chapter 12: Building a Complete Social Network PHP Web Application

In this chapter, we'll walk through the process of building a complete social network site from scratch. We'll start by outlining the key features and functionality that are essential to a social network, and then move on to the development process, including setting up a development environment, designing the database, building and testing the site, and finally, deploying it to a web server.

Throughout the project, we'll use best practices for secure coding and focus on performance optimization techniques to ensure that our social network site is fast, reliable, and secure. By the end of this chapter, you'll have a solid understanding of how to build a complete PHP web application and you'll be ready to take your skills to the next level.

12.1 Introduction to building a social network site

○ Purpose of building a social network site

In this chapter, you'll learn how to build a basic social network site from scratch. The purpose of this project is to demonstrate how to apply the PHP knowledge you've gained throughout the book to create a real-world web application. This project will cover various aspects of web development, including database design, user authentication and authorization, and working with forms.

○ What you will learn

By working through this project, you will gain hands-on experience in:

• Designing a database schema for a social network site

• Implementing user authentication and authorization

• Building user profiles and friend connections

• Creating posts and comments

• Displaying a news feed

• Working with forms and handling form submissions

○ What you need to know

Before you start, it is recommended that you have a solid understanding of PHP, HTML, CSS, and JavaScript, as well as a basic understanding of SQL and

and relational databases. If you need to brush up on any of these technologies, consider reviewing the relevant chapters in this book.

○ **The social network site specification**

For the purpose of this project, we will be building a basic social network site where users can:

• Register and login

• View their own profile and others' profiles

• Update their own profile information

• Add friends

• Create posts and comments on posts

• View a news feed of their friends' posts and comments.

This project will provide you with a strong foundation for building more advanced social network sites in the future.

12.2 Designing the database structure

Designing the database structure is a crucial step in building a social network site. In this subchapter, you will learn how to create a relational database that will store information about users, posts, comments, and relationships between users.

To start, you need to identify the main entities in the social network and their relationships with each other. For a simple social network, you can have the following entities:

• **Users**: This entity will store information about users who have registered on the social network, such as name, email, password, profile picture, etc.

• **Posts**: This entity will store information about posts made by users, such as text, date, and time of posting.

• **Comments**: This entity will store information about comments made on posts, such as text, date, and time of commenting.

• **Relationships**: This entity will store information about relationships between users, such as who is following whom.

With these entities in mind, you can create a relational database using SQL. Here's an example of how you can create the tables for the entities in the social network:

```sql
CREATE TABLE users (
  id INT AUTO_INCREMENT PRIMARY KEY,
  name VARCHAR(255),
  email VARCHAR(255) UNIQUE,
  password VARCHAR(255),
  profile_picture VARCHAR(255)
);

CREATE TABLE posts (
  id INT AUTO_INCREMENT PRIMARY KEY,
  user_id INT,
  text TEXT,
  date_time DATETIME,
  FOREIGN KEY (user_id) REFERENCES users (id)
);

CREATE TABLE comments (
  id INT AUTO_INCREMENT PRIMARY KEY,
  post_id INT,
  user_id INT,
  text TEXT,
  date_time DATETIME,
  FOREIGN KEY (post_id) REFERENCES posts (id),
  FOREIGN KEY (user_id) REFERENCES users (id)
);

CREATE TABLE relationships (
  id INT AUTO_INCREMENT PRIMARY KEY,
  follower_id INT,
  following_id INT,
  FOREIGN KEY (follower_id) REFERENCES users (id),
  FOREIGN KEY (following_id) REFERENCES users (id)
);
```

This is just a basic example, and you can add or modify the tables as per your requirements. With the database structure in place, you can start working on the application logic and the user interface.

12.3 Creating the user authentication and registration system

User authentication and registration system is an essential component of a social network site. It allows users to create an account, log in, and manage their profiles. The process of creating a user authentication and registration system involves the following steps:

• Designing the database table structure: The first step in creating the user authentication and registration system is to design the database table structure. The table should contain columns for storing the user's information, such as name, email address, password, and other relevant data.

• Implementing password hashing: For security reasons, it is recommended to store the user's password in a hashed format. You can use the password_hash function in PHP to hash the user's password before storing it in the database.

• Creating a registration form: You need to create a registration form where users can enter their information and create an account. The form should validate the user's input and ensure that the email address is unique.

• Inserting user data into the database: Once the form is submitted, you need to insert the user's information into the database. You can use the mysqli_query function in PHP to execute an INSERT query and store the user's data.

• Implementing login functionality: To allow users to log in, you need to create a login form where they can enter their email address and password. You can then verify the user's credentials by querying the database and comparing the submitted password with the hashed password stored in the database.

• Storing user information in a session: Once the user is successfully logged in, you need to store their information in a session. This allows you to keep track of the user's status and personalize the site for them.

• Logout functionality: You also need to implement a logout feature that allows the user to end their session and log out of the site.

By following these steps, you can create a user authentication and registration system that provides a secure and convenient way for users to create an account, log in, and manage their profiles.

Here's an example code for creating the user authentication and registration system in PHP:

```php
<?php
session_start();
```

```php
// connect to database
$host = "localhost";
$user = "your_username";
$password = "your_password";
$dbname = "your_dbname";

$conn = mysqli_connect($host, $user, $password, $dbname);
if (!$conn) {
    die("Connection failed: " . mysqli_connect_error());
}

// define registration function
function register() {
    global $conn;

    // get input values
    $username = $_POST['username'];
    $email = $_POST['email'];
    $password = $_POST['password'];
    $password2 = $_POST['password2'];

    // validate input values
    if (empty($username)) {
        $error = "Username is required";
    } elseif (empty($email)) {
        $error = "Email is required";
    } elseif (empty($password)) {
        $error = "Password is required";
    } elseif ($password != $password2) {
        $error = "Passwords do not match";
    } else {
        // check if username or email already exists
        $sql = "SELECT * FROM users WHERE username = '$username'
OR email = '$email' LIMIT 1";
        $result = mysqli_query($conn, $sql);
        if (mysqli_num_rows($result) > 0) {
            $error = "Username or email already exists";
        } else {
            // hash the password
            $password = password_hash($password, PASSWORD_DE-
FAULT);

            // insert data into the database
```

```php
            $sql = "INSERT INTO users (username, email, password)
VALUES ('$username', '$email', '$password')";
            if (mysqli_query($conn, $sql)) {
                $message = "Registration successful";
            } else {
                $error = "Error: " . $sql . "<br>" . mysqli_er-
ror($conn);
            }
        }
    }
}

// define login function
function login() {
    global $conn;

    // get input values
    $username = $_POST['username'];
    $password = $_POST['password'];

    // validate input values
    if (empty($username)) {
        $error = "Username is required";
    } elseif (empty($password)) {
        $error = "Password is required";
    } else {
        // check if username exists
        $sql = "SELECT * FROM users WHERE username = '$username'
LIMIT 1";
        $result = mysqli_query($conn, $sql);
        if (mysqli_num_rows($result) > 0) {
            // get the password hash
            $row = mysqli_fetch_assoc($result);
            $password_hash = $row['password'];

            // verify the password
            if (password_verify($password, $password_hash)) {
                // start the session
                $_SESSION['username'] = $username;

                // redirect to home page
                header("Location: home.php");
                exit();
```

Here's an example of the next steps for a user authentication and registration system in PHP:

```php
<?php
session_start();

// include database connection file
include_once 'db_connect.php';

// check if the form is submitted
if (isset($_POST['register'])) {
    // retrieve values from the form
    $username = mysqli_real_escape_string($conn, $_POST['user-name']);
    $email = mysqli_real_escape_string($conn, $_POST['email']);
    $password = mysqli_real_escape_string($conn, $_POST['password']);
    $confirm_password = mysqli_real_escape_string($conn, $_POST['confirm_password']);
    // check if passwords match
    if ($password != $confirm_password) {
        $_SESSION['message'] = 'Passwords do not match';
        header("Location: register.php");
        exit();
    }
    // hash the password for security
    $password = password_hash($password, PASSWORD_DEFAULT);
    // insert the new user into the database
    $query = "INSERT INTO users (username, email, password) VALUES ('$username', '$email', '$password')";
    if (mysqli_query($conn, $query)) {
        $_SESSION['message'] = 'User registered successfully';
        header("Location: login.php");
        exit();
    } else {
        $_SESSION['message'] = 'Error registering user';
        header("Location: register.php");
        exit();
    }
}
// close the database connection
mysqli_close($conn);

?>
```

Here is an example of how you could implement logout functionality in your social network site:

```php
<?php
session_start();

// destroy the current session
session_destroy();

// redirect to the login page
header("Location: login.php");
exit();
```

This code starts a session using the `session_start()` function, then destroys the current session using `session_destroy()`. Finally, it redirects the user to the login page using `header("Location: login.php")` and `exit()` to stop any further code execution.

Note that this is just one way of implementing logout functionality, and you can modify it to fit your specific needs.

12.4 Developing the User Profile Pages

In this section, we'll develop the user profile pages for our social network site. The user profile pages will show information about the user, such as their name, profile picture, and bio, as well as their friends and posts.

Here's an outline of the steps we'll follow to create the user profile pages:

• Create a new file, `profile.php`.

• Retrieve the user's information from the database.

• Display the user's information on the profile page.

• Display the user's friends and posts on the profile page.

Here's an example code implementation for the user profile page:

```php
<?php
// Start the session
session_start();

// Connect to the database
$db = mysqli_connect("localhost", "username", "password", "database_name");
```

```php
// Check if the user is logged in, otherwise redirect to the login
page
if (!isset($_SESSION['username'])) {
    header("Location: login.php");
    exit();
}

// Get the user's information from the database
$username = $_SESSION['username'];
$query = "SELECT * FROM users WHERE username='$username'";
$result = mysqli_query($db, $query);
$user = mysqli_fetch_assoc($result);

// Get the user's friends and posts from the database
$friends_query = "SELECT * FROM friends WHERE username='$user-
name'";
$friends_result = mysqli_query($db, $friends_query);
$friends = mysqli_fetch_all($friends_result, MYSQLI_ASSOC);

$posts_query = "SELECT * FROM posts WHERE username='$username'";
$posts_result = mysqli_query($db, $posts_query);
$posts = mysqli_fetch_all($posts_result, MYSQLI_ASSOC);

?>

<!DOCTYPE html>
<html>
<head>
    <title>Profile - <?php echo $user['username']; ?></title>
</head>
<body>
    <h1>Profile</h1>
    <p>Username: <?php echo $user['username']; ?></p>
    <p>Name: <?php echo $user['name']; ?></p>
    <p>Bio: <?php echo $user['bio']; ?></p>
    <h2>Friends</h2>
    <ul>
        <?php foreach ($friends as $friend) { ?>
            <li><?php echo $friend['friend_username']; ?></li>
        <?php } ?>
    </ul>
    <h2>Posts</h2>
    <ul>
```

```php
    <?php foreach ($posts as $post) { ?>
        <li><?php echo $post['content']; ?></li>
    <?php } ?>
  </ul>
</body>
</html>
```

In this example, we first retrieve the user's information from the database using a query and store the result in the `$user` variable.

Then, we retrieve the user's friends and posts from the database and store the results in the `$friends` and `$posts` arrays respectively.

12.5 Implementing the functionality for creating and managing posts

In this section, we will cover the implementation of the functionality for creating and managing posts on our social network site. The process of creating a post can be broken down into the following steps:

• Displaying the form for creating a post: We will create a form that allows users to enter a title, description, and image for their post. The form will be displayed on a dedicated page or as a modal on the user's profile page.

• Validation: Before the post is saved to the database, we need to validate the user's input. This can include checks for empty fields, length restrictions, and ensuring that an image has been uploaded if the user has chosen to include one.

• Saving the post to the database: If the user's input is valid, we will save the post to the database. This will include the title, description, image, and the user's ID who created the post.

• Displaying the posts: After the post has been saved to the database, we need to display it on the user's profile page, as well as on the home page. The home page should display a list of all posts created by the user's friends.

Here is an example code to create a post:
```php
<?php
    if (isset($_POST['create_post'])) {
        // get the post data
        $title = $_POST['title'];
        $description = $_POST['description'];
        $image = $_FILES['image']['name'];
        // validate the user's input
```

```php
        if (empty($title) || empty($description)) {
            $error = "Title and description are required fields";
        } elseif (strlen($title) > 100 || strlen($description) >
250) {
            $error = "Title must be less than 100 characters and
description must be less than 250 characters";
        } elseif ($image && !in_array(pathinfo($image, PATHINFO_
EXTENSION), array('jpg', 'jpeg', 'png'))) {
            $error = "Invalid image format. Only JPG, JPEG and PNG
are allowed.";
        }

        // if there are no errors, save the post to the database
        if (!isset($error)) {
            $query = "INSERT INTO posts (user_id, title, descrip-
tion, image) VALUES ('$user_id', '$title', '$description', '$im-
age')";
            if (mysqli_query($conn, $query)) {
                // redirect to the user's profile page
                header("Location: profile.php");
                exit();
            }
        }
    }
?>

<form action="" method="post" enctype="multipart/form-data">
    <div>
        <label for="title">Title:</label>
        <input type="text" id="title" name="title">
    </div>
    <div>
        <label for="description">Description:</label>
        <textarea id="description" name="description"></textarea>
    </div>
    <div>
        <label for="image">Image:</label>
        <input type="file" id="image" name="image">
    </div>
    <input type="submit" name="create_post" value="Create Post">
</form>
```

The above code implements the functionality for creating a new post by inserting it into the database and displaying it on the user's profile page.

To manage posts, we can add code for updating and deleting existing posts. For example, we can create two buttons for each post - one for editing and one for deleting - that trigger corresponding PHP functions.

Here is an example code for updating a post:

```php
// edit post
if (isset($_POST['edit_post'])) {
  $post_id = $_POST['post_id'];
  $post_body = $_POST['post_body'];

  // update post in database
  $query = "UPDATE posts SET post_body='$post_body' WHERE post_
id='$post_id'";
  $result = mysqli_query($conn, $query);

  if (!$result) {
    echo "Error updating post: " . mysqli_error($conn);
  }
}
```

And here is an example code for deleting a post:

```php
// delete post
if (isset($_POST['delete_post'])) {
  $post_id = $_POST['post_id'];

  // delete post from database
  $query = "DELETE FROM posts WHERE post_id='$post_id'";
  $result = mysqli_query($conn, $query);

  if (!$result) {
    echo "Error deleting post: " . mysqli_error($conn);
  }
}
```

Note that the code above assumes the existence of a database connection `$conn` and relevant tables in the database. It's important to implement proper error handling and security measures, such as sanitizing user input and using prepared statements, to prevent vulnerabilities and protect against attacks like SQL injection.

12.6 Building the functionality for adding and managing friends

In a social network site, the ability to add and manage friends is a crucial feature. In this section, we'll build the functionality for users to add new friends, accept friend requests, and remove existing friends.

First, we'll create a new database table called `friends` to store the relationships between users. The table will have three columns: `id`, `user1_id`, and `user2_id`. The `id` column will be the primary key for the table, and the `user1_id` and `user2_id` columns will store the IDs of the two users in each friendship.

Next, we'll create a form for users to search for other users by username and send friend requests. This form will have an input field for the username and a submit button. When the form is submitted, we'll search the database for the specified username and, if found, send a friend request from the current user to the specified user.

To implement the functionality for accepting and removing friends, we'll create two new pages: `friends.php` and `friend_actions.php`. The `friends.php` page will display a list of the user's current friends and any pending friend requests. The `friend_actions.php` page will be responsible for processing requests to accept or remove friends.

The code for accepting a friend request will look like this:

```
// check if the request is to accept a friend request
if (isset($_GET['accept'])) {
    $friend_id = $_GET['accept'];
    // add the friendship to the friends table
    $query = "INSERT INTO friends (user1_id, user2_id)
            VALUES ($user_id, $friend_id)";
    mysqli_query($conn, $query);
}
```

And the code for removing a friend will look like this:

```
// check if the request is to remove a friend
if (isset($_GET['remove'])) {
    $friend_id = $_GET['remove'];
    // remove the friendship from the friends table
    $query = "DELETE FROM friends
            WHERE (user1_id = $user_id AND user2_id = $friend_id)
            OR
```

```
                  (user1_id = $friend_id AND user2_id = $user_id)";
    mysqli_query($conn, $query);
}
```

Finally, we'll modify the `home.php` page to display the posts of the user's friends. To do this, we'll retrieve the IDs of the user's friends from the `friends` table and use those IDs to search for posts in the `posts` table. The resulting posts will be displayed on the `home.php` page.

12.7 Adding the Feature for Sending and Receiving Private Messages

Private messaging is a key feature in most social networking websites. It enables users to communicate directly with each other. In this section, we'll implement the functionality for sending and receiving private messages.

To start, we'll need to add a table to our database to store the messages. The table should have columns for the sender ID, the recipient ID, the message text, and the time the message was sent. Here's an example of what the table could look like:

```
CREATE TABLE messages (
    id INT(11) AUTO_INCREMENT PRIMARY KEY,
    sender_id INT(11) NOT NULL,
    recipient_id INT(11) NOT NULL,
    message TEXT NOT NULL,
    time_sent TIMESTAMP NOT NULL DEFAULT CURRENT_TIMESTAMP
);
```

Next, we'll create a page where users can view their messages. This page should display a list of messages with the sender's name, the message text, and the time the message was sent. The user should be able to reply to messages from this page as well. Here's an example of what the code for this page might look like:

```
<?php
    // Connect to the database
    $conn = mysqli_connect("localhost", "username", "password", "da-
tabase");

    // Get the messages for the current user
    $query = "SELECT messages.*, users.username FROM messages
              JOIN users ON messages.sender_id = users.id
              WHERE recipient_id = '{$_SESSION['user_id']}'
              ORDER BY time_sent DESC";
```

```php
$result = mysqli_query($conn, $query);

  // Display the messages
  while ($row = mysqli_fetch_array($result)) {
    echo "<p>From: {$row['username']}</p>";
    echo "<p>Message: {$row['message']}</p>";
    echo "<p>Sent: {$row['time_sent']}</p>";
    echo "<hr>";
  }

  // Display the form for sending a message
  echo "<form action='send_message.php' method='post'>";
  echo "<label for='recipient'>To:</label>";
  echo "<input type='text' name='recipient' id='recipient'>";
  echo "<label for='message'>Message:</label>";
  echo "<textarea name='message' id='message'></textarea>";
  echo "<input type='submit' value='Send'>";
  echo "</form>";
?>
```

And here is an example of how you could implement the functionality for sending messages in PHP:

```php
// create the page for sending messages
$sender_id = $_SESSION['user_id'];
$receiver_id = $_POST['receiver_id'];
$message = $_POST['message'];

// insert the message into the messages table in the database
$sql = "INSERT INTO messages (sender_id, receiver_id, message)
        VALUES ('$sender_id', '$receiver_id', '$message')";

if ($conn->query($sql) === TRUE) {
    // if the query was successful, redirect the user back to the
messages page
    header("Location: messages.php");
    exit();
} else {
    // if there was an error with the query, print an error mes-
sage
    echo "Error: " . $sql . "<br>" . $conn->error;
}
```

This code first gets the sender's id, receiver's id, and message from the form on the messages page. Then, it inserts the message into the messages table in the database using an INSERT statement. If the query was successful, the user is redirected back to the messages page. If there was an error with the query, an error message is printed.

12.8 Implementing the feature for creating and joining groups

Groups are an important aspect of many social networks, as they allow users to connect with others who share similar interests. To implement the feature for creating and joining groups, we will need to design the database structure, create the forms for creating and joining groups, and build the functionality to handle user actions.

First, we need to create a groups table in the database to store information about each group, such as the group name, description, and members. Here's an example of the structure of the groups table:

```
CREATE TABLE groups (
  id INT AUTO_INCREMENT PRIMARY KEY,
  name VARCHAR(255) NOT NULL,
  description TEXT NOT NULL,
  creator_id INT NOT NULL,
  date_created DATETIME NOT NULL
);
```

Next, we need to create a form for users to create a new group. This form should allow users to enter the group name, description, and select a group creator. The code for the form might look something like this:

```
<form action="create_group.php" method="post">
  <div class="form-group">
    <label for="group_name">Group Name</label>
    <input type="text" class="form-control" id="group_name"
name="group_name">
  </div>
  <div class="form-group">
    <label for="group_description">Description</label>
    <textarea class="form-control" id="group_description"
name="group_description"></textarea>
  </div>
  <div class="form-group">
    <label for="group_creator">Creator</label>
```

```
    <select class="form-control" id="group_creator" name="group_
creator">
        <?php
            // retrieve the list of users from the database
            $users = $db->query("SELECT * FROM users");
            while ($user = $users->fetch_assoc()) {
                echo "<option value='" . $user['id'] . "'>" . $user['us-
ername'] . "</option>";
            }
        ?>
    </select>
  </div>
  <button type="submit" class="btn btn-primary">Create Group</but-
ton>
</form>
```

We also need to create a form for users to join an existing group. This form should display a list of available groups and allow users to select the group they want to join. The code for the form might look something like this:

```
<form action="join_group.php" method="post">
  <div class="form-group">
    <label for="group">Group</label>
    <select class="form-control" id="group" name="group">
        <?php
            // retrieve the list of groups from the database
            $groups = $db->query("SELECT * FROM groups");
            while ($group = $groups->fetch_assoc()) {
                echo "<option value='" . $group['id'] . "'>" .
$group['name'] . "</option>";
            }
        ?>
    </select>
  </div>
  <button type="submit" class="btn btn-primary">Join Group</but-
ton>
</form>
```

Finally, we will implement the functionality for creating and joining groups. This will allow users to connect with others who have similar interests. To accomplish this, we will add a "Groups" section to the navigation bar, where users can create new groups, join existing ones, and view all of the groups they are a member of. Additionally, we will need to add a database table to store information about the groups, including the group name, description, and membership information.

12.9 Developing the news feed and notification system

In the social network site, it is important to have a news feed and notification system to keep users informed about the latest activities on the site. In this section, we will develop the functionality for the news feed and the notification system.

○ **News Feed**

The news feed is the main page of the social network site where users can see updates from their friends and the groups they belong to. The following steps outline the process for implementing the news feed functionality:

• Retrieve the posts from the database: We will retrieve the posts from the "posts" table in the database and store the results in an array.

• Filter the posts: We will use a loop to iterate through the array of posts and check if the post was created by a friend of the user or if the post was created by a member of a group that the user belongs to.

• Display the filtered posts: For each post that meets the criteria, we will display the post on the news feed page along with the author's name, the date the post was created, and the post's content.

Here is an example code for the news feed functionality in PHP:

```
// retrieve the posts from the database
$query = "SELECT * FROM posts";
$result = mysqli_query($conn, $query);

// initialize an array to store the filtered posts
$filtered_posts = array();

// loop through the results
while ($row = mysqli_fetch_assoc($result)) {
    // check if the post was created by a friend of the user
    $friend_query = "SELECT * FROM friends WHERE user_id = {$_SES-
SION['user_id']} AND friend_id = {$row['user_id']}";
    $friend_result = mysqli_query($conn, $friend_query);
    $is_friend = mysqli_num_rows($friend_result) > 0;

    // check if the post was created by a member of a group that
the user belongs to
    $group_query = "SELECT * FROM group_members WHERE user_id =
{$_SESSION['user_id']} AND group_id = {$row['group_id']}";
```

```php
    $group_result = mysqli_query($conn, $group_query);
    $is_group_member = mysqli_num_rows($group_result) > 0;

    // if the post was created by a friend or a member of a group,
add it to the filtered posts array
    if ($is_friend || $is_group_member) {
        $filtered_posts[] = $row;
    }
}

// display the filtered posts
foreach ($filtered_posts as $post) {
    echo "<h3>{$post['author']}</h3>";
    echo "<p>{$post['content']}</p>";
    echo "<p>{$post['date']}</p>";
}
```

○ **Notification System**

The notification system is a crucial aspect of a social network site, as it allows users to be alerted of new activity on the site, such as new posts, messages, or friend requests.

To implement the notification system, we need to create a notifications table in the database to store the notification details, including the type of notification, the user who triggered it, and the recipient.

Next, we need to update the relevant parts of the site's code to insert a new notification into the database whenever an event occurs that requires a notification, such as a new friend request or a new post.

We also need to create a page that displays the notifications for the logged-in user, and a way to mark them as read.

Here's an example of how the code for the notifications page could look:

```php
<?php
// Include database connection information
include 'db_connect.php';

// Start session
session_start();

// Get the user's ID from the session
$user_id = $_SESSION['user_id'];
```

```php
// Get the unread notifications for the user
$query = "SELECT * FROM notifications
          WHERE recipient_id = $user_id AND is_read = 0";
$result = mysqli_query($conn, $query);

// Fetch the results
$notifications = mysqli_fetch_all($result, MYSQLI_ASSOC);
?>

<!-- Display the notifications -->
<div class="notifications">
  <h2>Notifications</h2>
  <ul>
    <?php foreach ($notifications as $notification) : ?>
      <li>
        <?php echo $notification['message']; ?>
        <a href="mark_notification_as_read.php?id=<?php echo $no-
tification['id']; ?>">Mark as read</a>
      </li>
    <?php endforeach; ?>
  </ul>
</div>
```

And here's an example of the code for marking a notification as read:

```php
<?php
// Include database connection information
include 'db_connect.php';

// Get the ID of the notification to mark as read
$notification_id = $_GET['id'];

// Mark the notification as read
$query = "UPDATE notifications SET is_read = 1 WHERE id = $notifi-
cation_id";
mysqli_query($conn, $query);

// Redirect back to the notifications page
header("Location: notifications.php");
exit();
```

12.10 Deploying the social network site to a live web server

Deploying a web application to a live server is an important step in the development process as it makes the application accessible to a wider audience. In this section, we'll cover the steps to deploy our social network site to a live web server.

○ **Preparing the Site for Deployment**

Before deploying the site, it's important to make sure that it's ready for a live environment. This involves ensuring that the site is secure and the database is properly optimized. To prepare the site for deployment, follow these steps:

• Review the code for any vulnerabilities or security risks and make necessary changes.

• Remove any unnecessary code or commented out code that may affect the performance of the site.

• Optimize the database by indexing columns, reducing the size of tables, and removing unused data.

○ **Uploading the Site to the Live Server**

Once the site is ready for deployment, it's time to upload it to the live server. There are several ways to do this, including using a FTP client, using Git, or using an FTP uploader in your hosting account's control panel.

Here, we'll cover uploading the site to the live server using an FTP client. To do this, follow these steps:

• Connect to the live server using an FTP client, such as FileZilla or Cyberduck.

• Upload the site's files to the server, typically in a directory named "public_ html".

• Import the database to the live server.

• Update the database configuration file to reflect the live database credentials.

○ **Configuring the Live Server**

Once the site is uploaded to the live server, it's important to configure the server to work with the site. This may include setting up the database, configuring the PHP version, and updating the server's settings.

Here, we'll cover updating the database configuration file with the live database credentials. To do this, follow these steps:

• Open the database configuration file, typically named "config.php".

• Update the database host, username, password, and database name with the live server's credentials.

• Save the changes to the file.

○ **Finalizing Deployment**

Finally, we'll test the site on the live server to make sure that it's working as expected. To do this, follow these steps:

• Visit the site's URL in a web browser.

• Log in and test the site's features, including creating posts, adding friends, sending messages, and creating groups.

• Resolve any issues that may arise during testing.

With these steps, you have successfully deployed your social network site to a live web server and made it accessible to a wider audience.

Congratulations!

Chapter 13: Test your Knowledge

In this chapter, you'll have the opportunity to test your knowledge of PHP. The subchapter "13.1 Questions" will present 100 questions that cover a variety of topics related to PHP, including syntax, functions, database integration, and more. In "13.2 Answers", you'll find the answers to each question, along with explanations and additional resources to help you learn more.

This chapter is designed to help you gauge your understanding of the material covered in the previous chapters and identify areas where you may need further practice or study. Whether you're just starting out with PHP or you're looking to improve your skills, this chapter will provide a comprehensive review of what you've learned so far.

13.1 Questions

1. What is PHP and how does it work?

2. How does PHP differ from other programming languages?

3. What are the main benefits of using PHP for web development?

4. What is the syntax of PHP and how is it written?

5. What is the difference between PHP and HTML?

6. What is a PHP variable and how is it declared?

7. What is an array in PHP and how is it used?

8. What is a PHP function and how is it created?

9. How does PHP handle user input and form data?

10. What is the difference between single and double quotes in PHP?

11. How does PHP handle exceptions and error handling?

12. How does PHP handle cookies and sessions?

13. How does PHP interact with databases such as MySQL?

14. What is the PHP command line interface and how is it used?

15. How does PHP handle file and directory operations?

16. What is object-oriented programming in PHP and how is it implemented?

17. How does PHP handle security and protecting against attacks?

18. How does PHP handle file uploads and downloads?

19. What is the PHP mail function and how is it used?

20. What are some common PHP libraries and frameworks and how are they used?

21. What is a PHP class and how is it defined?

22. What is inheritance in PHP and how is it implemented?

23. What is polymorphism in PHP and how is it used?

24. What is an interface in PHP and how is it implemented?

25. How does PHP handle dates and time?

26. What is a PHP constant and how is it declared?

27. What are PHP regular expressions and how are they used?

28. What is a PHP closure and how is it implemented?

29. How does PHP handle file system and file permissions?

30. What is the difference between include and require in PHP?

31. How does PHP handle conditional statements and control structures?

32. What is a PHP loop and how is it implemented?

33. What are PHP switches and how are they used?

34. How does PHP handle mathematical and logical operations?

35. What is the PHP ternary operator and how is it used?

36. How does PHP handle arrays and array manipulation?

37. What is the difference between for and foreach loops in PHP?

38. What is the difference between the echo and print statements in PHP?

39. What are the different types of PHP arrays and how are they used?

40. How does PHP handle sorting and searching arrays?

41. What is a PHP string and how is it manipulated?

42. What are the different string functions available in PHP?

43. What is a PHP regular expression and how is it used?

44. How does PHP handle URL parsing and manipulation?

45. How does PHP handle HTTP requests and responses?

46. What is a PHP file and how is it manipulated?

47. What are the different file functions available in PHP?

48. What is a PHP directory and how is it manipulated?

49. What are the different directory functions available in PHP?

50. How does PHP handle XML processing and parsing?

51. What is a PHP SOAP client and how is it used?

52. How does PHP handle JSON processing and parsing?

53. What is a PHP curl library and how is it used?

54. What is the PHP get and post methods and how are they used?

55. What is the difference between $_GET and $_POST in PHP?

56. How do I use AJAX in PHP to dynamically update a page without reloading the whole page?

57. What is the difference between unset() and null in PHP?

58. How can I convert a date from one format to another in PHP?

59. How do I access the value of a GET request in PHP?

60. How can I prevent SQL injection attacks in PHP?

61. How do I make an HTTP request using PHP?

62. What is the PHP magic method __construct and how is it used?

63. How can I check if a variable is set or not in PHP?

64. How does PHP handle exceptions and error handling using trigger_error() function?

65. How can I return a value from a function in PHP?

66. How can I set a default value for a variable in PHP?

67. What is the difference between a session and a cookie in PHP?

68. How can I make a redirect in PHP?

69. How can I create a custom error page in PHP?

70. What is the difference between == and === in PHP?

71. How does PHP handle type casting and type juggling in variables?

72. How can I check if a string contains a specific word in PHP?

73. What is the difference between a static and a non-static method in PHP?

74. How can I concatenate strings in PHP?

75. How can I check the length of a string in PHP?

76. How can PHP be used to create and manage a database-driven website?

77. How can I check if a file exists in PHP?

78. How can I find the number of elements in an array in PHP?

79. How can I get the current date and time in PHP?

80. How can I extract data from a CSV file using PHP?

81. What is the difference between the while and do while loop in PHP?

82. How can I get the value of the current iteration in a for loop in PHP?

83. How can I remove duplicates from an array in PHP?

84. How can I get the value of a key in an associative array in PHP?

85. What is the difference between the array_map and array_walk functions in PHP?

86. How can I find the average of values in an array in PHP?

87. How can I split a string into an array in PHP?

88. What is the difference between the array_filter and array_reduce functions in PHP?

89. How can I get the first and last elements of an array in PHP?

90. How can I find the sum of values in an array in PHP?

91. How can I determine the type of a variable in PHP?

92. How can I check if a number is odd or even in PHP?

93. How can I find the minimum and maximum value in an array in PHP?

94. What is the difference between the in_array and array_search functions in PHP?

95. How can I change the value of an element in an array in PHP?

96. How can I get the current URL in PHP?

97. How can I check if a key exists in an array in PHP?

98. How can I convert a string to uppercase or lowercase in PHP?

99. How can we increase the execution time of a PHP script?

100. How can I convert a number to a string in PHP?

13.1 Answers

1. PHP stands for Hypertext Preprocessor and is a server-side scripting language used for creating dynamic web pages. When a user visits a PHP-based website, the server processes the PHP code and generates HTML or other output that is then sent to the user's browser.

PHP code is executed on the server and generates HTML, CSS, or JavaScript, which is then sent to the user's browser. When the user submits a form or clicks on a link, the browser sends a request to the server, which then executes the appropriate PHP code to handle the request. This way, PHP allows for the creation of dynamic, interactive websites that can respond to user input and change their behavior in real-time.

In short, PHP is a powerful tool for creating dynamic and interactive web pages, and it works by executing code on the server and generating the appropriate output to be sent to the user's browser.

2. PHP is different from other programming languages in several ways. Firstly, it is specifically designed for web development and is especially good at server-side scripting. Unlike languages like JavaScript, which is primarily client-side, PHP runs on the server and generates HTML or other outputs that are sent to the client. This makes PHP a great choice for building dynamic, data-driven websites. Secondly, PHP is an interpreted language, meaning that the code is executed directly, rather than compiled and executed as a separate binary file. This makes development faster and more flexible, as changes can be made to the code and immediately tested. Finally, PHP has a large, active user community and a vast array of libraries and tools available, making it a great choice for web developers who want to get up and running quickly with a proven solution.

3. The main benefits of using PHP for web development are:

• Open-source and free: PHP is an open-source language, which means that it is free to use, distribute, and modify. This makes it a popular choice for small businesses and individual developers.

• Cross-platform compatibility: PHP can run on a variety of operating systems, including Windows, MacOS, and Linux.

• Easy to learn: PHP has a simple syntax and is easy to learn, especially for developers who already have experience with other programming languages.

• Large community: PHP has a large community of users and developers, which means that there is a wealth of resources, tutorials, and forums available for developers to use.

• Integration with other technologies: PHP can easily be integrated with other technologies such as HTML, CSS, and JavaScript. It also has a number of frameworks, such as Laravel and Symfony, that make it easy to build complex web applications.

• Scalability: PHP is a scalable language, which means that it can handle large amounts of traffic and data. This makes it a good choice for building both small and large-scale web applications.

4. The syntax of PHP is similar to other programming languages such as C, Java, and Perl. PHP code is written within PHP tags, which are delimited by `<?php` and `?>`. Within the PHP tags, you can write statements, variables, expressions, and functions, and combine them to create a script.

A PHP script can contain HTML, JavaScript, and CSS, and can be used to generate dynamic web pages based on user input or database information. PHP code is executed on the server, and the output is sent to the browser as HTML. This allows PHP to generate dynamic web pages that can respond to user requests, access and modify data stored in databases, and perform a wide range of other tasks.

5. The main difference between PHP and HTML is that HTML is a markup language used to structure and display content on the web, while PHP is a server-side scripting language used to create dynamic web pages. HTML is used to define the structure and content of a web page, including text, images, and other elements, while PHP is used to add interactivity and other dynamic features to a web page, such as user input processing, database access, and more. HTML is executed on the client side, while PHP is executed on the server side and generates HTML code that is sent to the client. This means that the PHP code is processed and executed before the page is displayed to the user, while the HTML code is simply displayed to the user as it is.

6. A PHP variable is a container that stores a value. It is declared using the "$" symbol followed by the name of the variable. For example:

```
$name = "John Doe";
```

In this example, "name" is the name of the variable and "John Doe" is its value. In PHP, the value of a variable can be changed and re-assigned at any time, making it a dynamic aspect of the language. It is important to note that the name of a PHP variable must start with a letter or an underscore and can only contain letters, numbers, and underscores.

7. An array in PHP is a data structure that stores a collection of values, which can be of different data types, under a single variable name. Arrays in PHP can be of two types: indexed arrays and associative arrays.

Indexed arrays are arrays that use a numeric index to access the elements, where the index starts from 0. For example:
```
$fruits = array("apple", "banana", "cherry");
```

Associative arrays are arrays that use named keys to access the elements, where the key can be a string or an integer. For example:
```
$fruits = array("fruit1" => "apple", "fruit2" => "banana",
"fruit3" => "cherry");
```

Arrays are used to store multiple values in a single variable, and to perform operations like looping through the elements, adding new elements, removing elements, sorting elements, and so on.

8. A PHP function is a block of code that can be reused multiple times throughout a PHP script. It is created using the function keyword followed by a unique function name and a set of parentheses. Within the parentheses, you can specify any arguments that the function should accept. The code within the function is executed whenever the function is called. Functions help to modularize code and improve code readability and maintainability. The syntax for declaring a PHP function is as follows:
```
function functionName($arg1, $arg2, ...) {
    // code to be executed
}
```

You can call the function by using its name followed by parentheses, including any required arguments:
```
functionName($arg1Value, $arg2Value, ...);
```

9. PHP handles user input and form data by using various built-in functions, such as `$_GET`, `$_POST`, and `$_REQUEST`, to retrieve and process the data submitted by the user. The form data can be accessed through these superglobal

arrays and used to perform actions, such as storing the data in a database or using it to dynamically generate content on a web page. To ensure the security of the data, it's recommended to validate the user input before processing it. This can be done using various techniques such as using regular expressions, sanitizing the input, and using prepared statements when working with databases.

10. In PHP, there is a difference between single quotes (') and double quotes (") when declaring strings. Single quotes are slightly faster than double quotes, as they do not require PHP to parse the string for variables.

When using single quotes, the string is taken literally and any variables within the string will not be evaluated.

```
$name = "John";
echo 'My name is $name';  // Outputs: My name is $name
```

When using double quotes, PHP will evaluate any variables within the string.

```
$name = "John";
echo "My name is $name";  // Outputs: My name is John
```

So, it is recommended to use single quotes unless you need to include variables within your string.

11. PHP handles exceptions and error handling through the use of try-catch blocks and error reporting functions. In a try-catch block, code that might throw an exception is executed in the "try" section, and any exceptions that are thrown are caught and handled in the "catch" section. Error reporting functions, such as `error_reporting()` and `trigger_error()`, can be used to display or log error messages and control the reporting of errors in PHP. Additionally, the `set_error_handler()` function can be used to specify a custom error handling function. These tools allow developers to write robust and reliable PHP code by effectively handling and responding to errors and exceptions.

12. In PHP, cookies and sessions are two methods used to store user data on the server between requests. A cookie is a small piece of data stored on the user's computer by the browser. It can be used to remember the user's preferences or login information for a certain period of time. Cookies can be set, retrieved, and deleted using the `setcookie()`, `$_COOKIE`, and `setcookie()` functions in PHP.

Sessions, on the other hand, are a way to store data on the server that is specific to a user. Unlike cookies, session data is stored on the server and is not accessible to the client. When a user visits a website, a unique session ID is assigned to them, which is stored in a cookie on their computer. This session ID is used to retrieve the user's session data from the server. PHP uses the `$_SESSION` superglobal array to store session data. To start a session in PHP, you need to use the `session_start()` function. The session data is automatically deleted when the session ends, which is typically when the user closes their browser.

13. PHP interacts with databases, such as MySQL, through the use of PHP extensions such as the MySQLi extension or the PDO extension. These extensions provide functions and methods that allow developers to connect to a database, execute queries, and retrieve results. For example, the MySQLi extension provides the `mysqli_connect()` function to connect to a database and the `mysqli_query()` function to execute a query. Results can be retrieved using functions such as `mysqli_fetch_assoc()` or `mysqli_fetch_array()`. The PDO extension provides a similar set of functions, but allows developers to interact with multiple database management systems using a consistent interface. This makes it easier to switch from one database system to another without having to rewrite the code.

14. The PHP command line interface (CLI) is a way to run PHP scripts directly from the command line, without the need for a web server or browser. It is used for running scripts and programs in PHP, and can be used for tasks such as automation, testing, and batch processing. The PHP CLI allows developers to run scripts and test code without the need for a web server or browser, making it a useful tool for testing and debugging code. To use the PHP CLI, you need to have PHP installed on your system and be familiar with basic command line usage.

15. PHP provides various functions for handling file and directory operations, such as reading from and writing to files, creating and deleting files and directories, and managing permissions.

The basic functions for reading and writing files are `fopen()`, `fread()`, `fwrite()`, and `fclose()`. For example, the following code opens a file for writing, writes some text to the file, and closes the file:

```php
$file = fopen("example.txt", "w");
fwrite($file, "This is an example.");
fclose($file);
```

For creating and deleting files and directories, the functions `mkdir()` and `rmdir()` can be used. The `chmod()` function is used to change file permissions.

For working with directories, PHP provides functions such as `opendir()`, `readdir()`, and `closedir()`, which allow you to iterate over the contents of a directory.

For creating and deleting files and directories, the functions `mkdir()` and `rmdir()` can be used. The `chmod()` function is used to change file permissions.

For working with directories, PHP provides functions such as `opendir()`, `readdir()`, and `closedir()`, which allow you to iterate over the contents of a directory.

For database operations, PHP provides various functions and extensions, such as mysqli and PDO, that allow you to connect to, query, and manipulate databases.

16. Object-oriented programming (OOP) is a programming paradigm that uses objects and classes to design applications and computer programs. It provides a way of structuring and organizing code, making it more modular and easier to maintain. In PHP, OOP is implemented using classes and objects, with classes defining the properties and behaviors of objects. Properties represent the state of an object, while behaviors represent the actions that an object can perform. Classes can also inherit from other classes, allowing for the creation of hierarchical relationships between classes. This helps to reduce code duplication and improve code reuse. To use OOP in PHP, a class is declared using the "class" keyword, and objects are created from a class using the "new" keyword. Methods and properties can then be accessed using the "->" operator.

17. In PHP, security is an important aspect to consider when building web applications. To protect against attacks, PHP provides several security measures, including input validation and sanitization, password hashing, using secure connections (HTTPS), and limiting file uploads to trusted file types. Additionally, it is important to keep the PHP software and any PHP-based software (such as CMSs or frameworks) up to date to minimize security vulnerabilities. Other security measures include using prepared statements when interacting with databases to prevent SQL injection attacks, using proper authentication and authorization, and using encryption for sensitive data. It is also important to thoroughly test and debug PHP code to prevent any potential security vulnerabilities.

18. PHP provides the function `move_uploaded_file()` to handle file uploads from a form submission. The function takes the temporary location of the uploaded file and a target location as arguments, and moves the file from the temporary location to the target location. You can also add checks for the file size and type before uploading to ensure the uploaded file meets the required specifications.

For downloads, you can use the PHP function `readfile()` to read the contents of a file and send it to the user's browser for download. You can also specify the name of the downloaded file using the Content-Disposition header.

19. The PHP mail function is a built-in function in PHP that allows you to send emails from a PHP script. It uses the Simple Mail Transfer Protocol (SMTP) to send emails and requires a functioning email server. The basic syntax of the PHP mail function is as follows:

`mail($to, $subject, $message, $headers)`;

Where:

• `$to`: the email address of the recipient.

• `$subject`: the subject of the email.

• `$message`: the body of the email.

• `$headers`: additional headers such as the sender's email address, the content type, etc.

20. The PHP libraries and frameworks provide pre-written code and structures to simplify and streamline common programming tasks. Some of the most commonly used libraries and frameworks in PHP include:

• Laravel - A free, open-source PHP web application framework that uses the Model-View-Controller (MVC) architectural pattern.

• CodeIgniter - A lightweight PHP framework designed for building dynamic web applications with a focus on speed and simplicity.

• Symfony - A full-stack PHP framework that provides a set of reusable components and tools for building robust, scalable web applications.

• Yii - A high-performance PHP framework that uses the Active Record pattern for working with databases.

• CakePHP - A rapid development framework for PHP that uses convention over configuration to simplify web application development.

These libraries and frameworks can be used for a wide range of tasks such as managing databases, handling user input and form data, sending emails, uploading files, and much more. They provide a set of tools and abstractions that make it easier to develop web applications with PHP.

21. A PHP class is a blueprint for creating objects that define a particular set of attributes and behaviors. In object-oriented programming, a class acts as a blueprint for creating objects, and an object is an instance of a class. To define a class in PHP, the "class" keyword is used, followed by the name of the class and the definition of the class within a set of curly braces.

Within the class, properties and methods can be defined, which represent the attributes and behaviors of the objects created from the class.

22. Inheritance in PHP is a fundamental concept in object-oriented programming that allows objects of a derived class to inherit properties and behaviors from its parent class. It allows a new class to reuse the methods and attributes of an existing class without having to rewrite the code. This helps to promote code reusability, maintainability, and readability. Inheritance is implemented in PHP using the "extends" keyword, which is used to specify that a new class is inheriting from a parent class. The syntax for defining a derived class that inherits from a parent class is as follows:

```
class DerivedClass extends ParentClass {
  // class body
}
```

With inheritance, the derived class has access to all the methods and attributes of the parent class, unless they are declared as private. The derived class can also override or extend the methods of the parent class by declaring a new method with the same name in the derived class. This allows the derived class to have its own implementation of the method while still inheriting the properties and behaviors of the parent class.

23. Polymorphism is a concept in object-oriented programming (OOP) that allows objects of different classes to be treated as objects of a common class. In PHP, polymorphism is implemented through method overriding and method overloading. Method overriding allows child classes to provide a different implementation of a method that is already defined in the parent class. Method overloading allows multiple methods with the same name but different parameters to be defined within a single class. The correct method to be called is determined by the number and type of arguments passed to the method. Polymorphism is used to create more flexible and reusable code by allowing objects to behave differently in different contexts.

24. An interface in PHP is a contract between an object and the outside world that defines a set of methods that an object must implement. It is used to ensure that objects of different types can be used interchangeably, by enforcing a common set of methods that must be present in each object. To implement an interface in PHP, you first define the interface using the interface keyword, and then specify the methods that must be implemented in the interface. Then, any class that implements the interface must implement all of the methods defined in the interface, using the implements keyword.

25. PHP provides several functions for working with dates and time, including `date()`, `time()`, `strtotime()`, and `date_format()`. These functions allow developers to retrieve and manipulate date and time information, such as the current date and time, the number of seconds since the Unix epoch, and more.

For example, the `date()` function can be used to format the current date and time into a human-readable string, while the `strtotime()` function can be used to convert a string into a timestamp. The `date_format()` function can be used to format a timestamp into a specific format.

It's also possible to perform arithmetic operations with dates and times, such as adding or subtracting a certain number of seconds, minutes, or hours. This can be useful for calculating the difference between two dates, for example.

In addition to these basic functions, PHP also provides more advanced features for working with dates and times, such as support for time zones, daylight saving time, and more.

26. A PHP constant is a value that cannot be changed once it is set. It is declared using the `define()` function, which takes two arguments: the name of the constant and its value. The syntax for declaring a constant is as follows:

```
define("CONSTANT_NAME", "value");
```

It is common practice to use all capital letters for the name of the constant to indicate that it is a constant. Constants are useful for storing values that need to be used throughout the script, such as database configuration information or website URLs. Once a constant is declared, it can be referenced in the script by its name.

27. A PHP regular expression is a sequence of characters that define a search pattern. They are used to match and replace specific text within a string. PHP provides several functions that support regular expression operations, such as `preg_match()`, `preg_replace()`, `preg_split()`, and more. Regular expressions are useful for a wide range of tasks, such as validating input, searching and replacing text, and more. They can be particularly useful when working with large amounts of text or data.

28. A PHP closure, also known as an anonymous function, is a self-contained block of code that can be passed around as a value. It can be used as a callback function, or to create a small, reusable piece of functionality that can be used in various parts of a PHP application.

A closure is created using the function keyword, followed by a set of parentheses that contain any arguments the closure will accept, and a pair of curly braces that define the code that the closure will execute. The closure is assigned to a variable, and can then be invoked like any other function.

Here is an example of a simple PHP closure:

```php
$addition = function($a, $b) {
  return $a + $b;
};

echo $addition(2, 3); // Outputs: 5
```

In this example, a closure is created that takes two arguments and returns the sum of those arguments. The closure is assigned to the variable `$addition`, and can be invoked just like any other function.

29. PHP provides a variety of functions for handling file system operations, including reading and writing files, creating and deleting directories, and checking file and directory permissions. To handle file permissions, PHP has functions such as `chmod()`, `chown()`, and `chgrp()` which can be used to change the permissions of a file or directory. Additionally, PHP has built-in constants like 0755 and 0777 that represent common permission sets, making it easier to set permissions. When working with files, it's important to consider security concerns such as preventing unauthorized access and protecting sensitive information. To address these concerns, it's recommended to use file system functions with caution and to always check the return values for errors.

30. In PHP, include and require are both used to include the code from one PHP file into another. The main difference between them is how they handle failures. If a file specified in an include statement cannot be found or has an error, a warning will be generated, but the execution of the script will continue. On the other hand, if a file specified in a require statement cannot be found or has an error, a fatal error will be generated and the execution of the script will stop. In general, it's recommended to use require when the file being included is essential for the proper functioning of the script, and include when the file is optional or can be substituted by alternative code.

31. Conditional statements and control structures in PHP are used to control the flow of the program based on certain conditions. The most common control structures in PHP include:

• `If-else` statement: Used to execute a block of code if a condition is true, and another block of code if the condition is false. The syntax for an if-else statement is as follows:

```
if (condition) {
  // code to be executed if condition is true
} else {
  // code to be executed if condition is false
}
```

• `Switch` statement: Used to execute a block of code based on multiple conditions. The syntax for a switch statement is as follows:

```
switch (expression) {
  case value1:
    // code to be executed if expression is equal to value1
    break;
  case value2:
    // code to be executed if expression is equal to value2
    break;
  ...
  default:
    // code to be executed if no case is true
    break;
}
```

• `For` loop: Used to execute a block of code a specified number of times. The syntax for a for loop is as follows:

```
for ($i = 0; $i < count; $i++) {
  // code to be executed each iteration of the loop
}
```

• `While` loop: Used to execute a block of code as long as a condition is true. The syntax for a while loop is as follows:

```
while (condition) {
  // code to be executed as long as condition is true
}
```

• `Do-while` loop: Similar to the while loop, but the code block will always be executed at least once. The syntax for a do-while loop is as follows:

```
do {
  // code to be executed at least once
} while (condition);
```

32. A PHP loop is a control structure that allows the repeated execution of a block of code until a certain condition is met. There are several types of loops

in PHP including:

• `For` loops: A for loop is used to repeat a block of code a specified number of times. The loop's counter is initialized, then the condition is checked, and the code block is executed, then the counter is incremented or decremented until the condition is false.

• `While` loops: A while loop is used to repeat a block of code as long as a certain condition is true. The condition is checked before each iteration and the code block is executed only if the condition is true.

• `Do-While` loops: A do-while loop is similar to a while loop, but the code block is executed at least once before the condition is checked.

Here's an example of a `for` loop in PHP:

```php
for ($i = 0; $i < 10; $i++) {
    echo "The number is: $i <br>";
}
```

Here's an example of a `while` loop in PHP:

```php
$x = 0;

while ($x < 10) {
    echo "The number is: $x <br>";
    $x++;
}
```

Here's an example of a `do-while` loop in PHP:

```php
$x = 0;

do {
    echo "The number is: $x <br>";
    $x++;
} while ($x < 10);
```

33. A PHP switch statement is a control structure that allows a programmer to execute different code blocks based on a provided expression. It is a convenient way to specify multiple conditions in a more readable manner than using multiple if-else statements. The switch statement evaluates the expression and compares it to the different case statements provided. If a match is found, the code block associated with the case is executed. If no match is found, the default case code block, if provided, is executed. The switch statement ends with the break statement which prevents the next code block from being executed.

Here is an example of how to use a PHP `switch` statement:

```php
$day = "Monday";

switch ($day) {
  case "Monday":
    echo "Today is Monday.";
    break;
  case "Tuesday":
    echo "Today is Tuesday.";
    break;
  case "Wednesday":
    echo "Today is Wednesday.";
    break;
  default:
    echo "Today is another day.";
}
```

In this example, the switch statement evaluates the value of the `$day` variable. If the value is "Monday", the code block associated with the "Monday" case is executed and the output will be "Today is Monday."

34. In PHP, mathematical and logical operations can be performed using various arithmetic and comparison operators. For example, arithmetic operators such as addition (+), subtraction (-), multiplication (*), division (/), modulo division (%), and increment (++) can be used to perform mathematical operations. Comparison operators such as equal to (==), not equal to (!=), greater than (>), less than (<), greater than or equal to (>=), and less than or equal to (<=) can be used to compare values and produce boolean results (true or false).

PHP also provides various logical operators such as AND (&&), OR (||), and NOT (!) which can be used to perform operations on boolean values and produce more complex logical expressions. The `if-else` and `switch` statements can also be used to make decisions based on the results of these operations and control the flow of the program.

For example:

```php
$num1 = 10;
$num2 = 20;

$sum = $num1 + $num2;

if ($sum > 15) {
```

```
    echo "The sum is greater than 15";
} else {
    echo "The sum is less than or equal to 15";
}
```

35. The PHP ternary operator is a shorthand way to write an if-else statement in a single line. It allows you to evaluate an expression and return one value if the expression is true and another value if it is false. The syntax of the ternary operator is:

```
$result = (expression) ? value if true : value if false;
```

For example, the following `if-else` statement:

```
if ($a > $b) {
    $max = $a;
} else {
    $max = $b;
}
```

can be written as:

```
$max = ($a > $b) ? $a : $b;
```

36. Arrays in PHP are a data type that allows you to store multiple values in a single variable. They can be used to store data of different types including strings, integers, floats, and more. Arrays in PHP can be either indexed or associative. Indexed arrays are arrays with a numeric index, while associative arrays have keys that are assigned to values.

To declare an array in PHP, you can use the `array()` function or square brackets `[]`. You can access elements in an array using the index or key. You can also manipulate arrays using a variety of built-in functions such as `sort()`, `shuffle()`, `array_push()`, `array_pop()`, `array_shift()`, and `array_unshift()`. Here's an example of declaring and accessing an associative array in PHP:

```
$fruits = array("apple"=>"red", "banana"=>"yellow", "grape"=>"pur-
ple");
echo $fruits["apple"];
// Output: red
```

And here's an example of declaring and accessing an indexed array in PHP:

```
$numbers = array(1, 2, 3, 4, 5);
echo $numbers[2];
// Output: 3
```

37. The "for" loop in PHP is a traditional loop that allows you to repeat a block of code a specified number of times. It's syntax is as follows:

```php
for ($i = 0; $i < count($array); $i++) {
    // code to be executed
}
```

The `$i` variable is used as a counter and the loop will continue to execute as long as the condition `$i < count($array)` is true.

On the other hand, the foreach loop in PHP is used specifically for arrays and is used to loop through each value in an array. Its syntax is as follows:

```php
foreach ($array as $value) {
    // code to be executed
}
```

The `foreach` loop automatically loops through each value in the array without the need for a counter variable like the for loop. It is considered to be a simpler and more efficient way to loop through arrays in PHP.

38. The difference between the `echo` and `print` statements in PHP is minimal. Both are used to output data to the screen, but there are a few key differences between them:

• echo is slightly faster than print, as it has no return value.

• print can be used in expressions, whereas echo cannot.

• print returns 1, whereas echo does not return any value.

Other than these differences, both echo and print can be used interchangeably in most cases. However, it is recommended to use echo as it is faster and has no return value, making it the better choice for most applications.

39. PHP supports several types of arrays, including:

• Numeric arrays: An array with a numeric index, where each element is stored and accessed using a numeric key.

• Associative arrays: An array with a string index, where each element is stored and accessed using a string key.

• Multidimensional arrays: An array that contains one or more arrays as its elements. Each element of a multidimensional array can be either a simple value or another array.

• Array of objects: An array that contains objects of a certain class as its elements.

Each type of array is used depending on the requirements and the nature of the data being stored. For example, if you need to store a list of items with a specific order, you would use a numeric array. If you need to store key-value pairs, you would use an associative array. And if you need to store a group of arrays, you would use a multidimensional array.

40. In PHP, arrays can be sorted and searched using various built-in functions. Some of the commonly used functions include:

- `sort()`: sorts an array in ascending order

- `rsort()`: sorts an array in descending order

- `asort()`: sorts an array and maintains the index association

- `ksort()`: sorts an array by the key

- `arsort()`: sorts an array in descending order and maintains the index association

- `krsort()`: sorts an array in descending order by the key

- `usort()`: sorts an array using a user-defined function

- `array_search()`: searches for a value in an array and returns the key if found

- `in_array()`: searches for a value in an array and returns true if found.

These functions can be used to manipulate arrays in various ways, depending on the requirement. For example, to sort an array in ascending order, one can use the sort() function, as shown below:

```
$fruits = array("lemon", "orange", "banana", "apple");
sort($fruits);
```

41. A PHP string is a sequence of characters used to represent text in PHP. PHP provides a number of functions for manipulating strings, including concatenation, finding the length of a string, extracting substrings, replacing characters or substrings, converting between upper- and lowercase, and more. Some of the most commonly used string manipulation functions in PHP include `strlen()`, `substr()`, `str_replace()`, `strtolower()`, `strtoupper()`. These functions can be used to perform a wide variety of tasks, such as formatting text for display, validating user input, and generating dynamic content.

42. In PHP, there are many built-in string functions available for manipulating strings. Some of the most commonly used string functions include:

- strlen() - returns the length of a string.

- strpos() - returns the position of the first occurrence of a substring in a string.

- str_replace() - replaces all occurrences of a search string with a replacement string.

- substr() - returns a portion of a string.

- strtolower() - converts a string to lowercase.

- strtoupper() - converts a string to uppercase.

- trim() - removes whitespace or other characters from the beginning and end of a string.

- ltrim() - removes whitespace or other characters from the beginning of a string.

- rtrim() - removes whitespace or other characters from the end of a string.

- explode() - splits a string into an array based on a specified delimiter.

- implode() - joins elements of an array into a single string, using a specified delimiter.

- sprintf() - returns a formatted string.

These are just some of the many string functions available in PHP, each serving a specific purpose for string manipulation.

43. A PHP regular expression (regex) is a sequence of characters that define a search pattern. Regex is used to match and manipulate strings, such as to validate form data, extract information from a string, replace or delete substrings, and more. Regex can be written in a variety of ways in PHP, but are most commonly used with the `preg_` functions, such as `preg_match`, `preg_replace`, and `preg_split`. Regex patterns are defined within delimiters, usually forward slashes, and contain special characters and symbols to match specific patterns of characters. The combination of these symbols and characters allow regex to be highly flexible and powerful in string manipulation.

44. In PHP, URL parsing and manipulation can be achieved using various functions such as `parse_url()`, `parse_str()`, `rawurlencode()`, `rawurldecode()`, `urlencode()`, and `urldecode()`. The `parse_url()` function can be used to split a URL into its various components, such as the scheme, host, path, query string, and fragment. The `parse_str()` function can be used to parse a query string and store its variables as an array. The `rawurlencode()` and `rawurldecode()` functions can be used to encode and decode a URL string, respectively, without converting certain characters.

These functions provide a convenient way to

manipulate URLs in PHP and can be used to implement functionality such as redirects, URL rewriting, and parsing incoming URLs.

45. In PHP, HTTP requests and responses can be handled using a variety of methods, including using the cURL library, the `file_get_contents()` function, and the HTTP stream wrapper.

For example, to make an HTTP GET request using cURL, you can use the following code:

```php
$curl = curl_init();
curl_setopt_array($curl, array(
  CURLOPT_URL => "https://www.example.com/api/data",
  CURLOPT_RETURNTRANSFER => true,
  CURLOPT_ENCODING => "",
  CURLOPT_MAXREDIRS => 10,
  CURLOPT_TIMEOUT => 30,
  CURLOPT_HTTP_VERSION => CURL_HTTP_VERSION_1_1,
  CURLOPT_CUSTOMREQUEST => "GET",
));

$response = curl_exec($curl);
$err = curl_error($curl);

curl_close($curl);

if ($err) {
  echo "cURL Error #:" . $err;
} else {
  echo $response;
}
```

To send an HTTP response, you can use the `header()` function in PHP. For example, to send a JSON response, you can use the following code:

```php
header('Content-Type: application/json');
echo json_encode($data);
```

46. A PHP file is a text file that contains PHP code and is saved with the ".php" file extension. The PHP code in the file can be executed on the server to generate dynamic web content. PHP files can manipulate files on the server, access databases, and perform various other tasks. To manipulate a file in PHP, you can use built-in functions such as `fopen()`, `fread()`, `fwrite()`, and `fclose()`. These functions allow you to open a file, read its contents, write to it, and close it, respectively. The file system functions in PHP also allow you to create, delete,

and move files, as well as perform various other operations on them.

47. In PHP, there are a number of functions available for manipulating files, including:

- fopen() - opens a file

- fclose() - closes a file

- fread() - reads a file

- fwrite() - writes to a file

- file_get_contents() - reads the entire contents of a file into a string

- file_put_contents() - writes a string to a file

- filesize() - returns the size of a file

- file_exists() - checks if a file exists

- is_readable() - checks if a file is readable

- is_writable() - checks if a file is writable

- unlink() - deletes a file

- copy() - copies a file

- rename() - renames or moves a file

- filetype() - returns the type of a file

These functions allow you to read and write files, check if a file exists and if it is readable or writable, delete or copy files, and perform other file-related operations.

48. A PHP directory refers to a folder or a location on a file system. In PHP, directories can be manipulated using various functions such as `mkdir()`, `rmdir()`, `opendir()`, `closedir()`, etc. These functions allow you to create, delete, open, and close directories, respectively. You can also manipulate the contents of a directory, such as reading the names of files in the directory or changing the permissions of the directory.

49. PHP has several functions available for manipulating directories, some of the commonly used functions are:

- mkdir() - creates a new directory

- rmdir() - removes an empty directory

- chdir() - changes the current directory
- getcwd() - returns the current working directory
- opendir() - opens a directory for reading
- closedir() - closes a directory
- readdir() - reads the contents of a directory
- rewinddir() - rewinds the directory pointer
- scandir() - returns an array of the files and directories in a directory
- is_dir() - checks if a path is a directory or not.

50. PHP provides several functions to handle XML processing and parsing. Some commonly used functions include:

- SimpleXML: A simple and easy-to-use library that provides a simple and intuitive interface to parse XML data.

- DOMDocument: An in-built library in PHP that provides a way to load, manipulate and save XML data.

- xml_parser_create(): A function that creates a new XML parser and returns a resource handle to be used by other XML parsing functions.

- xml_parse(): A function that parses an XML document.

- xml_set_element_handler(): A function that sets the functions to be called when an opening and closing tag is encountered in the XML data.

- xml_set_character_data_handler(): A function that sets the function to be called when character data is encountered in the XML data.

These functions provide a comprehensive set of tools for processing and parsing XML data in PHP. With the help of these functions, developers can extract data from XML files, validate XML data, and perform various other operations.

51. A SOAP (Simple Object Access Protocol) client is a piece of software that allows a PHP application to communicate with a SOAP web service. PHP provides built-in support for SOAP, including a SOAP client, which can be used to send request messages to a SOAP server, and receive response messages. To use a PHP SOAP client, the PHP SoapClient class is used, which requires the URL of the SOAP web service, and any parameters required to be passed in the request. The client then sends a request message to the web service, and receives a response message, which can be used by the PHP application.

The response message can be in the form of an XML document, which can be processed using XML parsing functions in PHP.

52. JSON (JavaScript Object Notation) is a lightweight data interchange format that is easy for humans to read and write and easy for machines to parse and generate. PHP provides built-in functions for parsing JSON data and converting it into PHP arrays and vice versa.

The json_encode function is used to convert a PHP value (such as an array) into a JSON string. The json_decode function is used to convert a JSON string into a PHP value. For example:

```
$array = array("apple", "banana", "cherry");
$json = json_encode($array);

// Output: ["apple","banana","cherry"]
echo $json;

$new_array = json_decode($json, true);

// Output: Array ( [0] => apple [1] => banana [2] => cherry )
print_r($new_array);
```

In addition to encoding and decoding, PHP also provides several options for controlling the format of the JSON data, such as encoding numeric strings as numbers, setting indentation for human-readable output, and more.

53. The PHP cURL library is a collection of functions that allow PHP to transfer data to and from servers. It supports a variety of protocols including HTTP, HTTPS, FTP, and many more. It can be used to perform tasks such as sending HTTP requests, uploading files, downloading content, and more. To use the cURL library, you need to install the cURL extension for PHP, and then use the curl_init, curl_setopt, curl_exec, and curl_close functions to perform various cURL operations. The curl_setopt function is used to set various options for the cURL request, such as the URL to be requested, the HTTP method, the request headers, and more. The curl_exec function is used to execute the cURL request, and the curl_close function is used to close the cURL session.

54. The GET and POST methods are used to send data to a server for processing.

The GET method is used to retrieve data from a server. The data is sent as part of the URL, and is visible in the address bar of the browser. The GET method is usually used to retrieve information from a server, and is considered less secure because the data is visible in the URL.

The POST method is used to send data to a server for processing. The data is sent as part of the HTTP request, and is not visible in the URL. The POST method is usually used to submit data to a server, and is considered more secure because the data is not visible in the URL.

In PHP, the GET and POST methods can be used to retrieve data from a form. The data can be accessed using the $_GET and $_POST superglobals, respectively. For example, to access a form field named "name", you would use $_POST['name'].

55. The main difference between the $_GET and $_POST methods in PHP is the way they transmit data.

$_GET method is used to retrieve data from a form that has been submitted using the GET method. The data sent with the GET method is appended to the URL, making it visible to anyone. This method is typically used for simple requests and is limited in size.

$_POST method is used to retrieve data from a form that has been submitted using the POST method. The data sent with the POST method is not visible in the URL and is generally used for more secure and larger transactions.

In summary, the $_GET method is suitable for simple, small and non-sensitive data transactions, while the $_POST method is more secure and suitable for larger, sensitive data transactions.

56. AJAX in PHP can be used to dynamically update a page without reloading the whole page by sending an asynchronous HTTP request to a PHP script. The PHP script processes the request, performs any necessary computations, and returns a response in the form of data (usually in JSON format). The JavaScript code on the page then uses this response to update the page content.

Here's an example of how you might use AJAX in PHP:

• The user triggers an event, such as clicking a button, that sends an AJAX request to a PHP script.

• The JavaScript code sends the AJAX request using the XMLHttpRequest object or the jQuery.ajax() function.

• The PHP script receives the request, processes it, and returns a response in the form of data.

• The JavaScript code receives the response and updates the page content without reloading the whole page.

Here's a simple example using jQuery.ajax():

```
<button id="myButton">Get Data</button>
<div id="myDataContainer"></div>

<script>
$(document).ready(function() {
  $("#myButton").click(function() {
    $.ajax({
      url: "get_data.php",
      type: "post",
      dataType: "json",
      success: function(data) {
        $("#myDataContainer").html(data.message);
      }
    });
  });
});
</script>
```

In this example, when the button with the id "myButton" is clicked, an AJAX request is sent to the "get_data.php" script. The script returns a JSON-encoded response, which is then used to update the content of the "myDataContainer" div.

57. The unset() function in PHP is used to destroy a variable, while null is a special value that represents the absence of any value. When a variable is assigned null, it still exists but has no value assigned to it. unset() removes the variable completely, so it is no longer accessible. In other words, unset() completely removes a variable, while null simply gives it a null value.

58. In PHP, you can convert a date from one format to another using the date() and strtotime() functions. The strtotime() function takes a string representation of a date and time and returns a timestamp, which can then be formatted using the date() function. For example:

```
$original_date = "2022-01-01";
$timestamp = strtotime($original_date);
$new_date = date("d-m-Y", $timestamp);
```

In this example, the strtotime() function is used to convert the string "2022-01-01" into a timestamp, which is then passed as an argument to the date() function to format the timestamp into the desired format "d-m-Y".

59. In PHP, you can access the values of a GET request through the $_GET superglobal array. Each key in the $_GET array corresponds to the name of a query parameter in the URL, and its value is the value of the parameter. For example, if the URL is http://example.com?param1=value1&param2=value2, you can access the values of param1 and param2 as follows:

```php
$param1 = $_GET['param1'];
$param2 = $_GET['param2'];
```

Note that the keys in the $_GET array are case-sensitive, so if you have a query parameter named param1 in the URL, you should access it as $_GET['param1'], not $_GET['Param1'] or $_GET['PARAM1'].

60. SQL injection attacks can be prevented in PHP by using prepared statements and parameterized queries, also known as parameter binding. This method allows you to separate data from the SQL code and eliminates the risk of malicious input being interpreted as code.

Here's an example of how to perform a database query using a prepared statement:

```php
$conn = new mysqli("localhost", "user", "password", "database");

// Prepare the query
$stmt = $conn->prepare("SELECT * FROM users WHERE username = ?");

// Bind the parameters
$stmt->bind_param("s", $username);

// Set the value of the parameters
$username = "example_username";

// Execute the query
$stmt->execute();

// Get the results
$result = $stmt->get_result();

// Loop through the rows
while ($row = $result->fetch_assoc()) {
    // Do something with the data
}

// Close the statement
```

```
$stmt->close();

// Close the connection
$conn->close();
```

Using prepared statements and parameter binding is one of the best ways to protect against SQL injection attacks. Other methods include escaping user input, using strict data type validation, and limiting database permissions.

61. To make an HTTP request using PHP, you can use a library such as cURL or file_get_contents(). The cURL library provides a simple way to make HTTP requests and provides a lot of options for customization. Here's an example of making a GET request with cURL:

```php
<?php
// Create a cURL handle
$ch = curl_init();

// Set URL and other options
curl_setopt($ch, CURLOPT_URL, "http://www.example.com");
curl_setopt($ch, CURLOPT_HEADER, 0);
curl_setopt($ch, CURLOPT_RETURNTRANSFER, true);

// Grab URL and pass it to the browser
$output = curl_exec($ch);

// Close cURL resource, and free up system resources
curl_close($ch);

// Do something with the output
echo $output;
?>
```

file_get_contents() is a simpler way to make an HTTP request and is often used for quick and simple requests. Here's an example of making a GET request with file_get_contents():

```php
<?php
$output = file_get_contents("http://www.example.com");

// Do something with the output
echo $output;
?>
```

62. The __construct() method is a magic method in PHP that is called automatically when an object is created from a class. It is used to initialize object properties, establish database connections, or perform any other necessary setup for the object. The __construct() method has the same name as the class, and can take arguments that can be used to initialize object properties. The syntax for declaring a __construct() method in a PHP class is as follows:

```
class ClassName
{
    function __construct(argument1, argument2, ...)
    {
        // Code to initialize object properties
    }
}
```

When creating a new object, you can pass arguments to the __construct() method as follows:

```
$object = new ClassName(argument1, argument2, ...);
```

63. You can check if a variable is set or not in PHP using the isset() function. The isset() function takes a variable as its argument and returns TRUE if the variable is set and has a value other than NULL, and FALSE otherwise. For example:

```
$variable = "value";

if (isset($variable)) {
    echo "The variable is set.";
} else {
    echo "The variable is not set.";
}
```

64. In PHP, exceptions and errors can be handled using the trigger_error() function, which allows you to raise an error in your code. The trigger_error() function is useful when you want to handle an error in a specific way, or if you want to throw an exception to be caught and handled by a try-catch block.

The syntax for the trigger_error() function is as follows:

```
trigger_error(string $error_message, int $error_type);
```

where $error_message is the message that will be displayed as the error message and $error_type is the type of error being triggered. The available error types are E_ERROR, E_WARNING, E_NOTICE, E_USER_ERROR, E_USER_WARNING, and E_USER_NOTICE.

For example, you can use the `trigger_error()` function to trigger an error when a file cannot be opened:

```
$file = @fopen('file.txt', 'r');
if (!$file) {
    trigger_error('Cannot open file.', E_USER_ERROR);
}
```

65. In PHP, you can return a value from a function by using the "return" statement followed by the value you want to return. For example:

```
function sum($a, $b) {
  return $a + $b;
}

$result = sum(5, 10);
echo $result; // Output: 15
```

The function `sum()` takes two arguments $a and $b and returns the sum of those two numbers. When the function is called and the result is stored in the variable $result, it can then be printed using the echo statement.

66. You can set a default value for a variable in PHP by using the "or" operator. The syntax is as follows:

```
$variable = $value or $default_value;
```

In this example, if $value is not set, the value of $default_value will be assigned to $variable. If $value is set, it will be assigned to $variable.

You can also use the ternary operator to set a default value. The syntax is as follows:

```
$variable = isset($value) ? $value : $default_value;
```

In this example, if $value is set, it will be assigned to $variable, otherwise, $default_value will be assigned to $variable.

67. In PHP, a session and a cookie are both ways to store data on the client side, but there are some differences between them:

• Persistence: A cookie is stored on the client's computer and has an expiration date, whereas a session is stored on the server and lasts only for the duration of the user's visit.

• Security: Cookies can be accessed by any page on a website, and their data can be easily tampered with by the client. Sessions are stored on the server, making it more secure.

• Size: Cookies have a limited size of 4 KB, whereas sessions can store much more data.

• Use case: Cookies are best for storing small amounts of data, such as a user's preferences or a shopping cart. Sessions are best for storing more sensitive information, such as login credentials.

In summary, cookies are more suitable for storing data that needs to persist across multiple visits, while sessions are more suitable for storing temporary data that needs to be kept secure.

68. In PHP, you can make a redirect using the header() function. The header() function sends a raw HTTP header to the client, and the location header is used to redirect a user to a different URL. The syntax for a redirect using header() is as follows:

```
header('Location: http://www.example.com/');
exit;
```

It is important to note that the header() function must be called before any output is sent to the browser. If there is any output before the header() function call, the redirect will not work.

69. In PHP, you can create a custom error page by using a combination of the error reporting settings and the set_error_handler() function. Here is an example of how you can implement a custom error page in PHP:

First, set the error reporting level using the error_reporting() function. You can set the error reporting level to a specific value or use one of the predefined constants. For example, to report all errors except for notices, you can use:

```
error_reporting(E_ALL & ~E_NOTICE);
```

Next, define the custom error handler function using the set_error_handler() function. This function takes two arguments: the error level and the error message. For example:

```
function customErrorHandler($errno, $errstr) {
  // Display custom error page here
}
```

Finally, set the custom error handler using the set_error_handler() function. For example:

```
set_error_handler("customErrorHandler");
```

Now, when an error occurs, the custom error handler function will be called, and the custom error page will be displayed. Note that you can use the error_get_last() function to retrieve the last error that occurred and display it on your custom error page.

70. In PHP, the difference between "==" and "===" is in their comparison rules.

"==" compares the values of two variables and returns true if they are equal. This comparison is performed after type coercion, meaning that if the two variables have different types, PHP will attempt to convert one of them to the type of the other before comparing their values.

"===" compares the values and types of two variables and returns true only if both the value and type are equal. This comparison does not perform type coercion, meaning that if the two variables have different types, they will never be equal.

Therefore, "===" is often considered a stricter comparison operator than "==". It is generally recommended to use "===" in PHP code, especially when comparing values that have different expected types.

71. In PHP, type casting refers to converting a variable from one data type to another, while type juggling refers to the automatic conversion of data types in certain situations. PHP supports both implicit and explicit type casting.

Implicit type casting occurs automatically in some cases, such as when performing a comparison between variables of different data types, or when passing a variable to a function that expects a different data type.

Explicit type casting can be performed using type casting functions such as (int), (float), (string), (array), (bool), (object), and (unset). For example, (int) $var will cast the value of $var to an integer, and (string) $var will cast the value of $var to a string.

It's important to keep in mind that type casting may result in data loss or unexpected behavior, especially when converting between different data types that have different ranges or values.

72. In PHP, you can check if a string contains a specific word by using the strpos() function. The strpos() function returns the position of the first occurrence of a substring in a string. If the substring is not found, strpos() returns false.

For example, the following code will return the position of the first occurrence of "word" in the string "This is a test string":

```
$string = "This is a test string";
```

```php
$word = "word";

if (strpos($string, $word) !== false) {
    echo "The word '$word' was found in the string '$string'";
} else {
    echo "The word '$word' was not found in the string '$string'";
}
```

Alternatively, you can use the preg_match() function which uses a regular expression pattern to search for a match in a string. For example:

```php
$string = "This is a test string";
$word = "word";

if (preg_match("/$word/", $string)) {
    echo "The word '$word' was found in the string '$string'";
} else {
    echo "The word '$word' was not found in the string '$string'";
}
```

72. In PHP, a method can be either static or non-static.

A static method is a method that is called on a class rather than an instance of the class. This means that you do not need to instantiate an object from the class to call the method. Instead, you can call the method using the class name followed by two colons (::) and the method name. Static methods can access only static properties and cannot access non-static properties or methods.

A non-static method, on the other hand, is a method that is called on an instance of a class. This means that you need to create an object from the class to call the method. Non-static methods can access both static and non-static properties and methods.

Here is an example of a class with both static and non-static methods:

```php
class Example {
    public static $staticProperty = "This is a static property.";
    public $nonStaticProperty = "This is a non-static property.";

    public static function staticMethod() {
        echo self::$staticProperty;
    }

    public function nonStaticMethod() {
        echo $this->nonStaticProperty;
```

```
    }
}

Example::staticMethod(); // Output: This is a static property.

$example = new Example();
$example->nonStaticMethod(); // Output: This is a non-static prop-
erty.
```

74. In PHP, strings can be concatenated using the "." (dot) operator. For example:
```
$string1 = "Hello";
$string2 = "World";
$string3 = $string1 . " " . $string2;

echo $string3; // outputs "Hello World"
```

Alternatively, you can use double quotes to embed variables within a string:
```
$string1 = "Hello";
$string2 = "World";
$string3 = "$string1 $string2";

echo $string3; // outputs "Hello World"
```

75. The length of a string in PHP can be checked using the strlen function. Here's an example:
```
$string = "Hello, World!";
$length = strlen($string);
echo "The length of the string is: $length";
```

The above code would output: "The length of the string is: 13".

76. PHP can be used to create and manage a database-driven website by using a database management system (DBMS) such as MySQL, PostgreSQL, or SQLite. The PHP script can connect to the database using the appropriate extension (e.g. mysql, pgsql, or sqlite) and perform various operations such as inserting, updating, and retrieving data.

To perform these operations, you can use various functions such as mysqli_connect() to connect to the database, mysqli_query() to execute a SQL query, and mysqli_fetch_assoc() to retrieve data from the result set. You can also use an object-oriented approach with the PDO class.

Additionally, you can use PHP to handle user authentication and authorization, such as logging in and logging out, and restrict access to certain pages based on user role.

With these features, PHP can be used to build a dynamic and scalable website that utilizes a database for storing and retrieving data.

77. In PHP, you can check if a file exists using the file_exists() function. The function returns TRUE if the specified file exists and FALSE if it does not exist.

Example:

```php
$file = "example.txt";

if (file_exists($file)) {
    echo "The file exists";
} else {
    echo "The file does not exist";
}
```

78. In PHP, you can find the number of elements in an array using the count() function. Here is an example:

```php
$fruits = array("apple", "banana", "cherry");
$number_of_fruits = count($fruits);
echo "Number of fruits: " . $number_of_fruits;
//Output: "Number of fruits: 3"
```

79. In PHP, the date function is used to get the current date and time. The first argument to this function specifies the format of the date and time, while the second argument is a timestamp that defaults to the current time. Here's an example:

```php
$current_date_time = date("Y-m-d H:i:s");
```

The above example will return the current date and time in the format YYYY-MM-DD HH:MM:SS.

80. You can extract data from a CSV file using PHP by using the following code:

```php
<?php

$file = fopen("file.csv","r");

while(! feof($file))
{
  $data = fgetcsv($file);
```

```
    print_r($data);
}

fclose($file);

?>
```

This code opens a file named "file.csv" in read mode, reads its contents line by line using fgetcsv() function, and prints the data as an array.

81. The difference between while and do...while loop in PHP is the way the condition is evaluated:

• while loop: The condition is evaluated before each iteration of the loop. If the condition is false, the loop will not be executed.

```
$i = 1;

while ($i <= 5) {
    echo $i;
    $i++;
}
```

• do...while loop: The code block inside the loop is executed at least once, and then the condition is evaluated. If the condition is true, the loop continues to run.

```
$i = 1;

do {
    echo $i;
    $i++;
} while ($i <= 5);
```

In short, while loop is used when you want to repeat the loop only if a certain condition is met, whereas do...while loop is used when you want to repeat the loop at least once, and then check the condition to determine if the loop should continue to run.

82. You can get the value of the current iteration in a for loop in PHP by using the loop counter variable:

```
for ($i = 0; $i < 5; $i++) {
    echo "The value of the current iteration is: $i\n";
}
```

In this example, the loop counter variable $i represents the current iteration of the loop. It starts with a value of 0, increases by 1 after each iteration, and stops when its value is no longer less than 5.

83. You can remove duplicates from an array in PHP using the `array_unique` function:

```
$input = array("a" => "green", "red", "b" => "green", "blue", "red");
$result = array_unique($input);

print_r($result);
```

This code creates an array $input with duplicate values, and then removes the duplicates by calling the `array_unique` function. The resulting array is stored in the $result variable and can be printed using the `print_r` function.

Note that `array_unique` preserves the key association of the first occurrence of each value, so the resulting array may have different keys than the original array.

84. You can get the value of a key in an associative array in PHP using the following syntax:

```
$array = array("a" => "apple", "b" => "banana", "c" => "cherry");
$value = $array["a"];

echo $value;
```

In this example, the array $array is an associative array that maps the keys "a", "b", and "c" to the values "apple", "banana", and "cherry", respectively. The value of the key "a" can be accessed by using the square brackets [] and the key name. The value of the key is then stored in the variable $value and can be printed using the echo statement.

85. The `array_map` and `array_walk` functions are both used to process arrays in PHP, but they work in slightly different ways:

• array_map: This function maps a callback function to each element of an array and returns a new array with the modified elements. The function takes two arguments: the first is the callback function, and the second is the array to be processed.

```
$numbers = array(1, 2, 3, 4);
$squared = array_map(function($n) { return $n * $n; }, $numbers);

print_r($squared);
```

In this example, the `array_map` function is used to square each element of the $numbers array and returns a new array $squared with the modified elements.

• array_walk: This function is similar to `array_map`, but it modifies the elements of the original array directly instead of returning a new array. The function takes three arguments: the first is the array to be processed, the second is the callback function, and the third is an optional user-defined argument that can be passed to the callback function.

```
$numbers = array(1, 2, 3, 4);
array_walk($numbers, function(&$n) { $n = $n * $n; });

print_r($numbers);
```

In this example, the `array_walk` function is used to square each element of the `$numbers` array directly, modifying the original array.

In short, `array_map` returns a new array with modified elements, whereas `array_walk` modifies the elements of the original array directly.

86. You can find the average of values in an array in PHP using the `array_sum` function and dividing it by the number of elements in the array:

```
$numbers = array(1, 2, 3, 4);
$sum = array_sum($numbers);
$count = count($numbers);
$average = $sum / $count;

echo $average;
```

In this example, the `array_sum` function is used to calculate the sum of all elements in the $numbers array. The count function is used to find the number of elements in the array. The average is then calculated by dividing the sum by the count and stored in the variable $average. Finally, the average is printed using the echo statement.

87. You can split a string into an array in PHP using the explode function:

```
$string = "apple,banana,cherry";
$array = explode(",", $string);

print_r($array);
```

In this example, the string $string is split into an array using the explode function, which takes two arguments: the first is the separator (a comma in this case), and the second is the string to be split. The resulting array is stored in the variable $array and can be printed using the `print_r` function.

88. The `array_filter` and `array_reduce` functions are both used to process arrays in PHP, but they work in slightly different ways:

• `array_filter`: This function filters elements of an array based on a given condition. The function takes two arguments: the first is the array to be filtered, and the second is an optional callback function that defines the filtering condition.

```
$numbers = array(1, 2, 3, 4);
array_walk($numbers, function(&$n) { $n = $n * $n; });


print_r($numbers);
```

In this example, the `array_filter` function is used to filter out all odd numbers from the $numbers array and return a new array $evens with the even numbers.

• `array_reduce`: This function reduces an array to a single value by iteratively applying a callback function to each element of the array. The function takes two arguments: the first is the array to be reduced, and the second is the callback function.

```
$numbers = array(1, 2, 3, 4);
$sum = array_reduce($numbers, function($carry, $n) { return $carry + $n; }, 0);


echo $sum;
```

In this example, the `array_reduce` function is used to sum up all elements in the $numbers array and return the sum. The third argument 0 is an optional initial value that is used as the first argument to the callback function.

In short, `array_filter` filters elements of an array based on a given condition, whereas `array_reduce` reduces an array to a single value by iteratively applying a callback function to each element of the array.

89. You can use the following code to get the first and last elements of an array in PHP:

```
$array = [1, 2, 3, 4, 5];
$first_element = reset($array);
$last_element = end($array);
echo "First Element: $first_element";
echo "Last Element: $last_element";
```

In this code, the reset function is used to get the first element of the array, and the end function is used to get the last element of the array.

90. You can use the `array_sum` function to find the sum of values in an array in PHP. For example:

```php
$numbers = array(1, 2, 3, 4, 5);
$sum = array_sum($numbers);

echo "The sum of values in the array is: $sum";
```

This will return the sum of values in the $numbers array, which is 15.

91. You can use the gettype function to determine the type of a variable in PHP. This function returns the type of a variable as a string. For example:

```php
$num = 123;
$str = "Hello, World!";
$bool = true;
$arr = array(1, 2, 3, 4, 5);
$obj = new stdClass();

echo "Type of \$num: " . gettype($num) . "\n";
echo "Type of \$str: " . gettype($str) . "\n";
echo "Type of \$bool: " . gettype($bool) . "\n";
echo "Type of \$arr: " . gettype($arr) . "\n";
echo "Type of \$obj: " . gettype($obj) . "\n";
```

This will return the following output:

```
Type of $num: integer
Type of $str: string
Type of $bool: boolean
Type of $arr: array
Type of $obj: object
```

92. You can use the modulus operator (%) to check if a number is odd or even in PHP. The modulus operator returns the remainder of a division between two numbers. If the remainder is 0, the number is even; otherwise, the number is odd. For example:

```php
$num = 123;

if ($num % 2 == 0) {
    echo "$num is even.";
} else {
    echo "$num is odd.";
}
```

This will return the following output:

```
123 is odd.
```

93. You can use the min and max functions to find the minimum and maximum value in an array in PHP. For example:

```
$numbers = array(1, 2, 3, 4, 5);
$min = min($numbers);
$max = max($numbers);

echo "The minimum value in the array is: $min";
echo "The maximum value in the array is: $max";
```

This will return the following output:

```
The minimum value in the array is: 1
The maximum value in the array is: 5
```

94. The in_array and array_search functions are both used to search for a value in an array in PHP, but they have different return values and are used for different purposes.

in_array returns a boolean value indicating whether a given value is present in an array or not. It returns true if the value is found, and false if the value is not found.

For example:

```
$fruits = array("apple", "banana", "cherry");

if (in_array("apple", $fruits)) {
    echo "Apple is in the array.";
} else {
    echo "Apple is not in the array.";
}
```

This will return the following output:

```
Apple is in the array.
```

array_search returns the key of the first value in the array that matches a given value. If the value is not found in the array, it returns false. For example:

```
$fruits = array("apple", "banana", "cherry");
$key = array_search("banana", $fruits);
if ($key !== false) {
```

```
    echo "Banana is at key $key in the array.";
} else {
    echo "Banana is not in the array.";
}
```

This will return the following output:

```
Banana is at key 1 in the array.
```

95. You can change the value of an element in an array by accessing it using the index or key of the element, and then assigning a new value to it. For example:

```
$fruits = array("apple", "banana", "cherry");
$fruits[0] = "orange";

print_r($fruits);
```

This will return the following output:

```
Array
(
    [0] => orange
    [1] => banana
    [2] => cherry
)
```

96. You can use the $_SERVER superglobal array in PHP to get the current URL. Specifically, you can use the $_SERVER['REQUEST_URI'] variable.

For example:

```
$current_url = "http://" . $_SERVER['HTTP_HOST'] . $_SERVER['RE-
QUEST_URI'];

echo "The current URL is: $current_url";
```

This will return the current URL of the page, for example:

```
The current URL is: http://example.com/some/page.php
```

97. You can use the array_key_exists function in PHP to check if a key exists in an array. The function returns true if the specified key is found in the array, and false otherwise. For example:

```
$fruits = array("apple" => "red", "banana" => "yellow", "cherry"
=> "red");
```

```php
if (array_key_exists("apple", $fruits)) {
    echo "The key 'apple' exists in the array.";
} else {
    echo "The key 'apple' does not exist in the array.";
}
```

98. You can use the `array_key_exists` function in PHP to check if a key exists in an array. The function returns true if the specified key is found in the array, and false otherwise. For example:

```php
$fruits = array("apple" => "red", "banana" => "yellow", "cherry" => "red");

if (array_key_exists("apple", $fruits)) {
    echo "The key 'apple' exists in the array.";
} else {
    echo "The key 'apple' does not exist in the array.";
}
```

This will return the following output:
```
The key 'apple' exists in the array.
```

99. You can increase the execution time of a PHP script by setting the `max_execution_time` directive in the php.ini file. This directive sets the maximum amount of time, in seconds, that a script is allowed to run before it is terminated by the PHP interpreter.

For example, to increase the maximum execution time to 300 seconds, you would add the following line to your `php.ini` file:
```
max_execution_time(300);
```

You can also set the `max_execution_time` value programmatically in a script by using the `set_time_limit` function. For example:

```
set_time_limit(300);
```

Note that setting a high `max_execution_time` value may have security implications and is not recommended for production environments, as it can lead to resource exhaustion attacks. It is generally better to optimize your scripts to reduce their execution time, rather than increasing the maximum execution time.

100. In PHP, you can convert a number to a string by using the strval function or by concatenating the number with an empty string. For example:

```
$num = 42;

$string1 = strval($num);
$string2 = $num . "";

echo "String 1: $string1\nString 2: $string2";
```

This will return the following output:

```
String 1: 42
String 2: 42
```

Conclusion

Congratulations on reaching the end of this book on learning PHP!

You have covered a lot of ground in this journey, from setting up a local development environment to building a complete social network PHP web application. You have learned about PHP syntax and data types, functions, arrays, object-oriented programming, working with forms, database interaction, error handling, security, performance optimization, and deployment.

By following along with this book and practicing the examples provided, you should now have a solid foundation for building dynamic web applications using PHP.

However, this is just the beginning. To continue your learning journey, it is recommended to keep practicing and exploring more advanced topics. There are many resources available online, such as tutorials, forums, and online courses, where you can find additional information and expand your knowledge.

In conclusion, I hope that this book has provided you with the necessary tools and knowledge to start developing robust PHP web applications.

I wish you all the best in your future endeavors and hope that you continue to learn and grow in your programming journey.

www.ingramcontent.com/pod-product-compliance
Lightning Source LLC
LaVergne TN
LVHW051245050326
832903LV00028B/2573